THAILAND: SEVEN DAYS IN THE KINGDOM

Published and distributed by
Asia Books Co., Ltd
5 Sukhumvit Road Soi 61
Bangkok 10110, Thailand
P. O. Box 40
Tel. 391 2680, 391 0590
Fax. (662) 381 1621, 391 2277

© Times Editions Pte Ltd 1987
1 New Industrial Road
Singapore 1953

Designed by Viscom Design Associates, Singapore
Typeset by Koford Prints, Singapore
Color-separated by Far East Offset, Kuala Lumpur
Printed by Star Standard Industries Pte Ltd, Singapore
Photographs shot on Kodak film

ISBN: 9971-40-116-9

Endpapers: Cloth used for monks' robes.
Photographer: **Dominic Sansoni**, Sri Lanka

Facing page: His Majesty King Bhumibol
Adulyadej uses a camera regularly on his
frequent provincial trips.
Photographer: **Kraipit Phanvut**, Thailand

Pages 2-3: The canal at Damnern Saduak, in
Ratchaburi Province, is a busy artery of
communication, as well as the site of a noted
floating market.
Photographer: **Nik Wheeler**, Great Britain

Page 5: Two novices in a Chiang Mai temple —
almost every Thai man enters a monastery at
some time in his life, usually just before he
marries and starts a family of his own.
Photographer: **Dominic Sansoni**, Sri Lanka

Pages 6-7: Wat Prathat Lampang Luang in the
northern province of Lampang is framed against
a sunset-filled sky.
Photographer: **Ping Amranand**, Thailand

Pages 8-9: Mist swirls over the forested slopes of
Doi Mae Salong in the north.
Photographer: **Leong Ka Tai**, Hong Kong

Pages 10-11: As day begins, two fishermen set
out into Phang Nga Bay in southern Thailand.
Photographer: **Andris Apse**, New Zealand

Pages 12-13: The incomparable beauty of a
fully-opened lotus blossom, one of the
principal emblems of the Buddhist faith.
Photographer: **John Everingham**, Australia

Pages 14-15: Blue-shirted mahouts teach their
great gray students a lesson at the Young
Elephant Training Center in Lampang, an
institution unique to Thailand. The school
closes in March for a three-month holiday.
Photographer: **John Everingham**, Australia

THAILAND

*S*EVEN *D*AYS IN THE *K*INGDOM

Photographed by **Kraipit Phanvut**, Thailand.

Nik Wheeler

Ping Amranand

THAILAND

SEVEN DAYS IN THE KINGDOM

Photographed by Fifty of the World's Great Photographers
During the Week of March 2-9, 1987

Text by William Warren
With a Foreword by Gore Vidal

AB
ASIA BOOKS

Leong Ka Tai,

Contents

o much happens in a week that when one has ended, we hardly remember how it began. On these pages, the first week of March 1987—or Minakhom 2530 on the Thai calendar—has been lovingly re-created in color and in black-and-white, with such a broad brush and at the same time in such fine detail that it will not fade from memory for many Thai moons to come.

The fifty photographers who had the good fortune and the great skill to freeze these warm Thai moments forever will never forget their contribution. The rest of us can only marvel at what they did and feast our eyes on what they saw through the lens. Their work is proof that seven days in Thailand is not like seven days in any other place on this planet we call Earth.

An Ancient Equilibrium

As photographs speak for themselves and William Warren speaks for himself in this most perceptive look at Thailand, I shall speak for — or rather to — the Eleventh Edition of the *Encyclopedia Brittanica* (Volume XXV), published in 1911. The entry for "Siam", as Thailand was known then, is the work of one Walter Armstrong Graham, Adviser to His Siamese Majesty's Minister for Agriculture. Previous to that, he had been a member of the Burma Civil Service, and before that, a professor of English History, in England. Otherwise, he is unknown to history. But his characteristically English survey of Siam is not too unlike that of the dread Anna Leonowens, authoress of *The English Governess at the Siamese Court.*

Mr. Graham describes the country; then he remarks on the inhabitants and their history. According to the first census (1905-09), there were 6,230,000 people, of whom a tenth lived in Bangkok. The government is an absolute monarchy. There are ten ministers of state, of whom agriculture ranks tenth. Happily, "most departments have the benefit of European advisers" like Mr. Graham. Despite the recording-angel style of the *Brittanica,* Mr. Graham's own voice keeps breaking in: "The numerous palace and other functions make some demand upon the ministers' time, and, as the king transacts most of his affairs at night, high officials usually keep late office hours." There is a note of self-pity here; and one can almost hear Mrs. Graham's incredulous voice, "Walter, it is three in the morning! Don't tell me you were at the palace all this time, discussing copra!"

But Walter would have us believe that he is beyond carnal temptation. "The typical Siamese," he writes, "is of medium height, well-formed, with olive complexion, darker than the Chinese, but fairer than the Malays, eyes well-shaped though slightly inclined to the oblique, nose broad and flat, lips prominent, the face wide across the cheekbones and the chin short.... The lips are usually deep red and the teeth stained black from the habit of betel-chewing. The children are pretty but soon lose their charm, and the race, generally speaking, is ugly from the European standpoint." Plainly, Walter prefers the moss-green teeth of Victorian England to Siam's elegant betel-black. One can also imagine the poignant moment when a parent is obliged to inform a child, "You have just lost your charm. It is over. We must be resigned." But then, "they are a light-hearted, apathetic people, little given to quarreling or to the commission of violent crime." So unlike the battling Westerners. It is here that Mr. Graham gives himself away with a single word: "Apathetic."

What Mr. Graham and most Westerners take to be Thai apathy is the Buddhist non-confrontational approach to life, which is totally unlike that of those who worship the Judeo-Christian God, forever in dubious battle on the plains of Heaven with Lucifer. Because of this constant rage in Heaven, we tend to mirror it on Earth where it is taken for granted that nation must constantly fight nation, class class, family family, and — the core of our literature, each member of a family is arrayed against the other ("Orestes! Come to Mother!"). Although the Thai Buddhists have had their share of wars and incursions, crimes and alarums, they cope with needless pain in ways different from ours. The Buddha teaches that pain comes from desire. Therefore, to eliminate desire is to lessen the pain of existence. Obviously no one lives up to this system any more than anyone has ever lived up to the tenets of Judaism or of Christianity, but a society based on the teachings of the Buddha is bound to be very different from one based upon a furious God dueling with a wily Devil.

In the three score and sixteen years since Mr. Graham noted, disparagingly, Thai "apathy", the unrelenting war of the West against not only man but nature itself has infected the planet. Sensibly, the Thais have tried to take what is necessary for them to survive without ever surrendering their ancient equilibrium, with its profound sense of a multitude of spirits in a world that is nothing but a series of illusions, on the order of a kaleidoscope. "All things are brief as winks", they believe, and each travels in "the little ferryboat" toward, if the passenger is enlightened, a shining state of wholeness. Meanwhile, for those of us still on the scene, the Buddha indicates a middle way or, as he is said to have said, "as the ocean has only one flavor, the flavor of salt, so has my doctrine only one flavor — the flavor of emancipation from sorrow," which comes from "thirst" or desire. The rest of what he teaches is our old friend ethics, familiar to all and ignored by most, Easterner and Westerner alike.

Thailand is the only important Southeast Asian society never to have been colonized by Westerners. Plainly, the maintenance of Buddhist "apathy" required — and still requires — a good deal of vigilance and cunning. But no matter what one's beliefs or non-beliefs, there is something universally reassuring in this essentially Buddhist society that continues to renew itself, like the lotus as it rises from the mud at the bottom to the water's surface.

— **Gore Vidal**

Old and New Looks at the Thai Kingdom

The kingdom of Siam — as remote and exotic as China or Japan — first made a real impression on the West at the end of the 17th century, thanks to a series of inquisitive Frenchmen who crossed the world to call at its capital of Ayutthaya. They were not the first Europeans to spend time in the kingdom; the Portuguese sent an envoy to the capital in 1511, shortly after they seized Malacca, and a number of nations had been attracted by Siam's wealth to establish "factories," or trading posts, outside Ayutthaya's massive walls, joining resident Chinese, Japanese, Malays, and Persians to make the Siamese capital one of the most cosmopolitan cities in the vast region now known as Southeast Asia.

But the Frenchmen who came between 1660 and 1688 were different from these earlier emissaries, whose primary concern lay in making money. They were more observant, more literate, and though they failed in their mission of converting King Narai to Christianity and establishing a powerful French presence, they nevertheless gave the world its first really revealing glimpses into the kingdom's life through the accounts many of them wrote upon returning to Europe.

One was the Abbé de Choisy, a Jesuit priest appointed by Louis XIV to a distinguished embassy headed by the Chevalier de Chaumont in 1685. De Choisy had an eccentric past, having been, in his youth, a celebrated transvestite in Parisian

Left: Wat Arun (the Temple of Dawn) and the Chao Phya River, taken around 1899; in the foreground can be seen some of the floating houses that once lined the river.
Above: King Chulalongkorn (Rama V) was the first Thai ruler to travel abroad; the kingdom was extensively modernized during his rule.

The Golden Mount (Wat Sakhet), for many
years the highest point in Bangkok, was begun
during the reign of King Rama III and
completed in that of King Rama V. Below is a
shot of a Bangkok *klong* around the turn of the
century; note the rickshaw, which first
appeared on the city streets in 1871.

society; he was also a perceptive traveler, who sought to share with his readers the exhilarating discoveries he made on his journey.

Imagine the kind of impression the elegant and erudite Frenchman must have made on his fellow countrymen and European intellectual circles when he wrote of his travels in the Siamese capital:

"I stood frequently in admiration of the strong great city, seated upon an island round which flowed a river three times the size of the Seine. There rode ships from France, England, Holland, China and Japan, while innumerable boats and gilded barges rowed by sixty men plied to and fro. No less extraordinary were the camps of villages outside the walls inhabited by the different nations who came trading there, with all the wooden houses standing on posts over the water, the bulls, cows, and pigs on dry land. The streets, stretching out of sight, are alleys of clear running water. Under the great green trees and in the little houses crowd the people. Beyond these camps of the nations are the wide rice fields. The horizon is tall trees, above which are visible the sparkling towers and pyramids of the pagodas. I do not know whether I have conveyed to you the impression of a beautiful view, but certainly I myself have never seen a lovelier."

Residential Bangkok in the early 20th century was mostly along *klongs* like this one.

Overleaf: This elephant roundup took place in a kraal just outside Ayutthaya, photographed in 1900. The pavilion at the back was built for the King and his guests.

Beautiful views the Abbé certainly conveyed, along with many intimate details of life in the city. Indeed, since almost all of Ayutthaya's historical documents were lost in the destruction of the capital by the Burmese a century later, much of our knowledge concerning its ordinary existence comes from such contemporary European accounts. Simon de la Loubère, for instance, who headed another mission two years after de Choisy, wrote an even more comprehensive work about his observations, in which he meticulously recorded what he learned about everything from local medical practice to the customs of polygamy, and every modern historian has drawn upon it to recreate the period.

Of pre-Ayutthayan Siam these outsiders knew almost nothing; nor, probably, did their royal hosts know much more, since this was a subject that did not receive serious attention until comparatively recent times. Neither, for example, knew that an advanced civilization had flourished in the northeastern part of the country as far back as 6,000 years ago, numbering among its achievements what some scholars regard as the world's first bronze metallurgy. Nor, in the European accounts at least, is there any mention of Sukhothai, established in 1238 and regarded as the first truly independent Thai kingdom.

The Thais, most historians believe, began migrating from southern China in the early part of the Christian Era. At first they formed a number of city states in the northern part of the country, in places like Chiang Saen, Chiang Rai, and Chiang Mai, but these were never strong enough to exert much influence outside the immediate region. Further south the broad and fertile Central Plains came to be dominated by the powerful Khmer empire, which lay to the east, and to a lesser extent by the Mons, whose kingdom was centered in Lower Burma.

This changed when several Thai chieftains united at Sukhothai to found a kingdom that was short-lived but of immense cultural importance in the nation's history. It was here that the first evidence of written Thai was left, along with distinctively Thai styles of art and architecture, which survived after Sukhothai was absorbed by the kingdom of Ayutthaya at the end of the 14th century.

Even lacking a knowledge of this eventful past, the French visitors made a vital contribution to history with their accounts of Ayutthaya at the peak of its power and influence. As it turned out, theirs was the last outsider's view for over a century. In 1688, conservative elements at King Narai's court took advantage of the ruler's illness to engineer a revolution, and nearly all foreigners disappeared from the scene as the kingdom entered a long period of isolation culminating in war with Burma.

The great Seated Buddha, Phra Mongkon Bopit, at Ayutthaya; the arm was broken off when the city was burnt in 1767. In 1951, a building was constructed to shelter the image.

A European painter at work in the compound of
Bangkok's Wat Po, noted for its porcelain
decorations. Below this picture is a
klong in old suburban Bangkok.

Readers in the West once more became aware of the country during the 19th century, when colonial expansion and a fresh interest in Far Eastern trade brought a new generation of diplomats and businessmen up the Chao Phya River to Bangkok, which had been established as the capital in 1782. Sir John Bowring, who came in 1855 to negotiate a historic treaty with King Mongkut (Rama IV), spent scarcely a month in the kingdom; but he had prepared himself by reading everything available and, while there, observed the scene around him with an eye every bit as curious as de Choisy's or de la Loubère's. The result was *The Kingdom and People of Siam,* a comprehensive work that included not only a sensitive portrait of King Mongkut and an account of the treaty discussions but also an encyclopedic store of minutiae on such matters as magic amulets, capital punishment, popular amusements, hair styles, and marriage customs. The following observations on Thai hospitality reveal both local mores and Bowring's own unbiased outlook:

"One of the courtiers told me that the King has mentioned my fondness for fruits; and the consequence was that many spontaneous offerings were brought to the palace, and found their way to my table. These are true courtesies, which I could only the more appreciate, as we had been given to understand that we should witness nothing but cold ceremonials, extorted urbanities, and a proud and repulsive policy. We were led to expect that we should find rapacity intrusive, insatiable, and extortionate, — every art employed to obtain much, and to give little in return. Far different was my experience. It seemed as if nothing was expected from me, while upon me and around me every kindness was profusely and prodigally showered. Even the children brought their garlands, which they hung on our arms; coronals of fragrant flowers, fresh roses, were every morning upon my table, In great things as in small, I found a hospitality that was almost oppressive, and of which I retain the most grateful memory."

Revealing as these accounts were, essential as they still are in providing a human dimension to official chronicles of wars, rulers and revenues, an element of romance nonetheless lingered in the absence of realistic visual evidence of Thai daily life. The etchings that illustrated early French accounts were fairly faithful in depicting plants and architecture, but they tended toward high fantasy when it came to people, showing statuesque Thais in poses that prefigured Rousseau's noble savage. Those in Bowring's work were more accurate, but few of them showed ordinary people and they lacked the sense of immediacy that appeared toward the end of King Mongkut's reign with the advent of photography in the kingdom.

Two of the sons of King Chulalongkorn,
probably attired for their tonsure ceremony.

The larger picture shows members of a
dance troupe in costume for a performance,
while below are a couple of monks from
the reign of King Rama V.

In the picture on top, a train stops at a provincial railway station, while the horse-drawn carriages, below, probably belong to the late 19th century.

A splendid parade welcomes King
Chulalongkorn back from one of his trips
abroad; on the left can be seen the walls of the
Grand Palace.

Among the first skilled practitioners of the new art was an Englishman named John Thomson, who arrived from Singapore in the autumn of 1865 and soon afterwards applied through the British consul to photograph the royal palace. This request was quickly granted; moreover, the King, who was deeply interested in Western inventions, appointed a day for his own picture to be taken.

"His Majesty entered through a massive gateway," Thomson wrote, "and I must confess that I felt much impressed by his appearance, as I had never been in the presence of an appointed sovereign before. He stood about five feet eight inches, and his figure was erect and commanding, but an expression of severe gravity was settled on his somewhat haggard face. His dress was a robe of spotless white, which reached right down to his feet; his head was bare. I was admiring the simplicity and purity of this attire, when His Majesty beckoned to me to approach him, and informed me that he wished to have his portrait taken as he knelt in an attitude of prayer."

While Thomson was making preparations, his royal subject suddenly changed his mind and left the room. He reappeared to pose first "in a sort of French Field Marshal's uniform" and later in his court robes. Proper positioning raised delicate problems, for Thomson had been warned that it was forbidden to touch either the King or his clothes, but his apprehension proved groundless. "Do what you require for the excellency of your photograph," King Mongkut told him.

The results — bearing no resemblance whatever to Yul Brynner's portrayal of the ruler in *The King and I* — were a great success. The King was so pleased he invited Thomson back to the palace in January 1866, to photograph the grand six-day ceremony that celebrated the cutting of the future King Chulalongkorn's top-knot. In his account of this, Thomson manages to get in a dig at Anna Leonowens, whose fanciful memoirs were to form the basis of the Broadway musical: "Among other photographs which I took on the spot, one represents His Majesty as he receives his son and places him on his right hand, amid the simultaneous adoration of the prostrate host. Mrs Leonowens, who ought to have known better, has made use of this photograph in a work on Siam which recently appeared under her name, and described it wrongly as 'Receiving Princess'."

Thomson's work was not limited to royal subjects. He also went up to the ruins of Ayutthaya, where he was almost trampled by an elephant when an assistant suddenly opened an umbrella to make the animal assume a more dramatic pose, and then, in the company of the American missionary Dr. Dan Beach Bradley, south to Phetchaburi, where he took some of the first pictures of rural Thai life.

The top portrait is of King Mongkut (Rama IV), during whose reign the first photographs were taken in the kingdom, while the lower one is King Rama VI, his grandson, who reigned from 1910 to 1925.

The top picture was taken in 1911, during the
cremation ceremonies that were held for King
Chulalongkorn (Rama V); the lower one shows
the coronation of his son, the future Rama VI.

Four native beauties in costumes of the day,
taken by a studio photographer; no dates are
given, but the pictures were probably made in
the early years of the present century.

This group of Bangkok ladies are dressed in
cowboy outfits, possibly inspired by early silent
films while, in the picture below, a theatrical
troupe poses with masks and musical instruments.

Use of the camera increased rapidly in the following reign, producing not only remarkably informal views of life in the royal palace — queens and concubines romping in the garden and the King dandling his favorite offspring on his knee — but also an increasing number of glimpses of life beyond such exalted circles. Compared with that of many other countries, however, Thailand's photographic record remained sparse. Problems of transportation, plus the cumbersome equipment required in early days, limited the average cameraman to the sights of Bangkok and the surrounding countryside. It was not until fifty years or so ago that photographers began to capture the kingdom as a whole, the mundane as well as the postcard picturesque.

Like the products of de Choisy, de la Loubère, and Bowring, the present work has a historical aspect in that it seeks to capture a specific moment in Thai life: namely, the first week of March in 1987. The record this time, however, is almost entirely pictorial. The participating photographers were given assignments extending throughout the kingdom, but besides covering particular aspects, they were encouraged to turn their lenses on whatever struck them as revealing about the ways Thais of 1987 earned a livelihood, worshipped, governed their country, enjoyed themselves; in brief, how they lived, at all levels of a varied society.

This is what they found.

Above: Life drifts on along a *klong* in turn-of-the-century Bangkok.
Right: A barefoot postman delivers the mail to a Bangkok house; the cropped hair was typical of Thai women of the end of the 19th century.

The Architecture of Thai Authority

"Head of the Thai people, supreme in rank, I draw comfort from your protection. Because of your gracious care all the people are happy and peaceful. We pray that whatever you wish for, fate will grant you according to your heart's desire, to bring you prosperity. We salute you!"

The words of the Thai royal anthem, performed at most official ceremonies and before the start of every movie, may strike a Western ear as somewhat archaic. After all, the system of absolute monarchy ended in 1932, following a revolution staged by a small group of disaffected civil servants and military men. Since then Thai kings have ruled under a constitution, their powers theoretically no greater than those of the few surviving crowned heads of Europe.

Yet the sentiments expressed in the anthem are a precise reflection of feelings held by nearly every Thai with regard to King Bhumibol Adulyadej the Great, the ninth ruler of the Chakri Dynasty founded some two centuries ago. Since he was officially crowned in 1950, King Bhumibol has assumed the role of constitutional monarch and has worked tirelessly on behalf of his people, gaining in the process a measure of personal devotion that is probably more intense than that felt for any of his all-powerful ancestors. Of the several institutions that form the foundation of modern Thai life, the one he personifies is not only the most visible but also the most revered.

Preceding pages: Statues of past Chakri Kings stand in the Royal Pantheon.
Photographer: **Luca Invernizzi Tettoni,** Italy

Left: A senior priest chants from the Buddhist scriptures at the cremation of a monk
Photographer: **Rio Helmi,** Indonesia

Photographer (above): **Paul Chesley,** United States

King Bhumibol has achieved this largely through a remarkable degree of direct contact with his subjects. In addition to his official residence in Bangkok, he maintains others in every part of the country, from Chiang Mai in the north to Narathiwat in the far south, and for at least eight months of the year he and his family — Queen Sirikit, Crown Prince Maha Vajiralongkorn, Princess Maha Chakri Sirindhorn, and Princess Chulabhorn — travel almost continuously throughout the provinces, overseeing assorted rural development projects.

These tours are conducted with a minimum of the ceremonial splendor that surrounds many of his ritual Bangkok appearances. The King merely selects a rural community and arrives, sometimes by helicopter but more often by car, boat, or even on foot. Once there, he talks informally with local people to learn their problems and, if possible, suggest solutions. Out of such discussions have come a wide range of "royally-suggested" schemes. These include reservoirs and irrigation systems for drought-plagued regions, drainage of swamps, artificial rain-making, cooperative farms, and scores of new crops to boost rural living standards. Still other projects have been initiated by members of King Bhumibol's family. Queen Sirikit, for instance, has led in the revival of traditional handicrafts as an alternative source of income, and the Princess Mother, now in her eighties, tirelessly leads medical teams to remote provinces where modern doctors are still rarely posted.

Activities of this sort have given the Thai monarchy a status possibly unique in the contemporary world. In part it is based on the traditional respect accorded to rulers ever since the Sukhothai kingdom; even more, though, it is due to esteem for King Bhumibol, who despite his constitutional limitations has managed to establish a moral authority that is perhaps all the more potent for being unwritten.

Buddhism is another of Thailand's fundamental institutions, with the Supreme Patriarch as head of the faith in the kingdom. Though freedom of belief extends to other religions and there are substantial minority groups of Muslims, Christians, and Hindus, the great majority of Thais follow Buddhist teachings, which have played a highly significant role in shaping social behavior over the centuries.

Official power rests with the government, personified by the Prime Minister, Parliament, and a bureaucratic system that reaches down to the village level. In the past few decades, the Prime Minister's personal power has steadily increased, largely because of the Thai tendency to express their concerns to the highest-ranking authority, in nation as well as family, with the result that provincial delegations frequently appear at Government House requesting decisions on local problems.

Students in Phetchaburi, outside Wat Mahatat, watch as their country's flag is raised.
Photographer: **Mark Howard,** Great Britain

Legislative power is vested in the Parliament, consisting of the elected House of Representatives and the Senate appointed by the King. The Parliament must approve all legislative matters of national policy, which then require the King's signature before becoming the law of the land.

The ministerial system controling the Thai bureaucracy is substantially the same today as the one created by reform-minded King Chulalongkorn (Rama V) in the 19th century, the only major addition being the Office of the Prime Minister. The largest and most powerful ministry is Interior, under whose auspices come a wide range of responsibilities, from provincial government to the police department, reaching down to the villages at the base of the pyramidal government structure.

The Thai armed forces, with the King as Head, consist of the Army, Navy, and Air Force, governed by the Supreme Command Headquarters. All young men are required to report for a military medical examination on reaching the age of twenty, and those who pass draw lots to determine whether they serve for a two-year period. Career officers generally graduate from one of three military schools with high physical as well as academic standards.

Since 1932, military leaders have figured prominently in Thai affairs. Sometimes their influence has been wielded openly, leading to coups d'état and the emergence of "strong men"; in recent years, however, it has tended to be more subtle and, as a consequence, more difficult for outsiders to fully comprehend. The primary duty of the armed forces, of course, is defense of the kingdom, and in this capacity they have waged a successful campaign against communist insurgents in several regions and maintained security along the border areas, sharing the latter responsibility with the Border Patrol Police. At the same time, the military exerts a political force, which is most apparent in its steadfast support of traditional Thai institutions.

One contemporary problem that comes partly under military supervision is that of Indochinese refugees, over a million of whom have come to Thailand since the communists took over their homelands in 1975. While many have since been resettled in host countries, a large number remain in camps near the borders, creating both political and economic problems for the kingdom.

The Thai flag, known as the *trai-rong* (three colors), can be seen as a symbol of the forces from which the kingdom derives its strength. Two bands of red, at top and bottom, represent the nation, while two white bands suggest the purity of the Buddhist faith; in the center, a blue band, filling a third of the total area, symbolizes the monarchy, still a vital element after seven centuries.

An evening ceremonial lowering of the flag takes place outside the Ministry of Defense in Bangkok. *Photographer:* **Leonard Lueras,** United States

His Majesty King Bhumibol Adulyadej spends most of each year overseeing various royal projects throughout the country. On visits to remote communities, he talks with villagers about their needs and consults with experts about solutions. The King is shown here in the Doi Saket district of Chiang Mai Province on a trip accompanied by an invited group of journalists.

Photographer: **Kraipit Phanvut,** Thailand

Below: His Majesty King Bhumibol Adulyadej has won the affection of his subjects through his tireless efforts to better their life through a wide variety of royally-sponsored projects, some of which are conducted on the grounds of Chitrlada Palace, the royal residence in Bangkok. Here he is shown talking to officials at a plant which produces powdered milk in the palace compound, while Her Royal Highness Princess Maha Chakri Sirindhorn takes notes on the proceedings.
Photographer: **Luca Invernizzi Tettoni**, Italy

Right (top and center): During the week the photographers were in the kingdom, His Royal Highness Crown Prince Maha Vajiralongkorn, heir to the Thai throne, was representing the King on an official visit to China. The event was widely covered in the local mass media, among them the *Bangkok Post,* which ran these pictures of the Crown Prince with Deng Xiaoping and at the Great Wall.
Photographs courtesy of the **Bangkok Post**

Right: Her Royal Highness Princess Maha Chakri Sirindhorn talks with one of the participants at a ceremony. All the royal children participate in the King's projects.
Photographer: **Luca Invernizzi Tettoni, Italy**

From his early student days in Switzerland, His Majesty King Bhumibol Adulyadej has been a keen photographer, and one of his favorite subjects is the beautiful Queen Sirikit. These two portraits of the Queen are reproduced by royal permission.
Photographer: **His Majesty King Bhumibol Adulyadej**

Left: A boat-shaped throne stands in the Amarindra Vinitchai Hall, where early rulers of the Chakri Dynasty gave royal audiences. The King entered from a door at the rear, after which the curtains were dramatically opened to reveal him sitting in state.

Above: An elegant bronze figure, richly decorated in the style of early Bangkok art, holds the sword of a past King in the Dusit Maha Prasat. The small picture shows the Niello Throne which stands in the Throne Hall of the Chakri Maha Prasat in the palace compound. Here the King receives the credentials of foreign ambassadors.

Photographer: **Luca Invernizzi Tettoni**, Italy

Above: Vimanmek, often described as the largest teak structure in the world, was built as a palace by King Rama V in the early years of the present century. Long neglected, it was restored to its former splendor by Her Majesty Queen Sirikit for the celebration of Bangkok's Bicentennial. This is the King's study while the small picture shows the Thai-style bedroom of Queen Saowapha Pongsri.

Right: A view of Vimanmek showing the delicate Victorian woodwork.

Photographer: **Luca Invernizzi Tettoni**, Italy

Left: A scene in the mile-square compound of the Grand Palace. The building in the background, called the Chakri Throne Hall, was built in the 1880s by the fifth Chakri King. It reflects an effort to combine Thai and Western styles of architecture.
Photographer: **Luca Invernizzi Tettoni,** Italy

Above: A soldier stands guard in Bangkok's Grand Palace before a pair of carved wooden doors that display his counterparts of two centuries ago.
Photographer: **Paul Chesley,** United States

Overleaf: Youthful participants go through their paces in a paramilitary display in Hat Yai. Patterns are formed when the devices they hold are turned around.
Photographer: **Richard Kalvar,** United States

Below: Commander in Chief of the Royal Thai Army, General Chavalit Yongchaiyudh pays his respects to the Supreme Patriarch of Thailand at Wat Rajabopit on the occasion of the Patriarch's 89th birthday.
Photographer: **Richard Kalvar,** United States

Right (top): Prime Minister Prem Tinsulanonda (left) chairs a meeting; Interior Minister General Prachuab Suntrangkul is on the right.
Photographer: **Richard Kalvar,** United States

Right (center): Dr. Ukrit Monkolnawin, President of the National Assembly, receives visitors at his office in the Parliament.
Photographer: **Barrie Rokeach,** United States

Right: General Pichitr Kullavanijaya, an important military leader, visits an agricultural development station in Kanchanaburi Province.
Photographer: **Richard Kalvar,** United States

Left: The military plays an important role in Thailand, not only in national defense but also in politics and social development. The current Commander in Chief of the Royal Thai Army is General Chavalit Yongchaiyudh, who assumed the post in 1986. He is reviewing the naval forces at Songkhla in the southern part of Thailand.
Photographer: **Richard Kalvar,** United States

Above: Naval forces present arms during the show of military power.
Photographer: **Barrie Rokeach,** United States

Above: An instructor makes a point using a real cobra.

Right: Thai army cadets undergo rigorous training in various parts of the country. These men are at a special Warfare Command Camp in Lopburi, an important military center near Ayutthaya.

Below: Admiral Supa Gajaseni, the Supreme Commander of Thailand's military forces, observes pre-cadet training exercises at the Fort Tanarat Infantry Center in Prachuap Kirikhan Province on the Gulf of Thailand.

Photographer: **Richard Kalvar,** United States

Overleaf: More than a million refugees have flocked to Thailand since Indochina fell to the communists in 1975. Here rice rations are being distributed at the Khao I Dang camp to some of the thousands who are still waiting to be resettled in host countries.
Photographer: **Ian Berry,** Great Britain

Ian Berry

Above: In Site 8, a camp containing some
30,000 Cambodian refugees and run by the
Khmer Rouge, children participate in a play
depicting the history of the Red Cross, whose
founder appears in the background.
Photographer: **Ian Berry**, Great Britain

Above: One of the numerous children in Site 8 plays with a canteen.

Below: A provisional hospital serves the sick at Site 2, a camp with a population of 152,000 run by the Khmer People's National Liberation Front. Though located in Thailand, it has the second largest concentration of Cambodians after Phnom Penh.
Photographer: **Ian Berry,** Great Britain

Overleaf: Monks stand in the ornately decorated doorway of the Viharn at Wat Phra That Lampang Luang, not far from the provincial capital of Lampang.
Photographer: **Ping Amranand,** Thailand

Ping Amranand

The Power of Beliefs

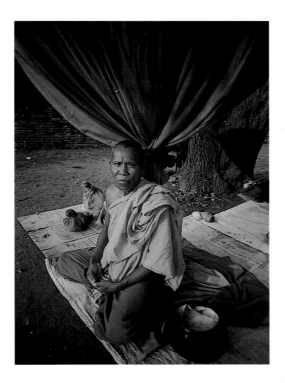

Along with the broad rice field, the most characteristic feature of the Thai scene is the fanciful outline of a Buddhist *wat:* the steep roof seeming to strain gracefully toward the sky, adorned with symbolic embellishments that often glitter with gold and glass mosaics in the sunlight. There are some 27,000 of these remarkable structures in the kingdom, and they offer impressive visual evidence of the faith followed by 95 per cent of the population.

Theravada Buddhism came to Thailand over a thousand years ago, brought by missionary monks from India. The Buddhist way was adopted by the Mons and later by the Thai King Ramkamhaeng (1275-1317), who made it the dominant religion of his capital at Sukhothai. It was here that the first great Thai temples rose. Chiang Mai's rulers built their grand monuments to Buddhism 500 years ago, but the increasingly magnificent edifices that earned merit for royal builders reached a peak of splendor in those of late Ayutthaya and early Bangkok. Countless artisans lavished their skills on these incredible monuments to faith, of which Somerset Maugham commented, "It makes you laugh with delight to think that anything so fantastic could exist on this somber earth."

But it is not in architecture, however striking, that Buddhism has made its most significant contribution to Thai culture. Its tolerant precepts, ideally suited to the

Left: Kanchanaburi Province has a "Floating Nun" who meditates while floating in a pool. Older Thai women often crop their hair and adopt the white robes of piety.
Photographer: **Bill Wassman,** United States

Photographer (above): **Steve Vidler,** Great Britain

native character and also allowing the assimilation of other beliefs and influences, have enabled it to pervade almost every aspect of life, with the result that in both monastery and marketplace it governs behavior in countless subtle ways.

Ordination into the Buddhist priesthood is one of the basic steps in attaining maturity for Thai men, from the King himself down to the humblest farmer. Indeed, in rural areas, one who has not served as a monk is known as a *khon dip*, an unripe person, and few girls would consider marriage to such a social misfit. Most enter the monastery for a limited period, a few weeks for the average city dweller, three months during the rainy season for villagers. Around a quarter of a million, however, have elected to stay a much longer time, in some cases for life, and with this brotherhood rests the responsibility of maintaining the faith in its more visible manifestations.

Though governed by a strict code of monastic discipline, involving obedience to 227 rules of personal behavior, Thai Buddhist monks nonetheless enjoy a considerable degree of freedom in practicing their religion. Some seek spiritual insight through meditation in deeply private places, while others — perhaps the majority — lead remarkably active lives, traveling about freely except during the annual Rains Retreat and coming into frequent contact with the world outside the monastery. Most leave the *wat* daily to collect alms from neighboring laymen, who thereby earn merit. In addition, they preach sermons on Buddhist sabbath days, write philosophical articles and books, and, in groups, participate by chanting prayers at all sorts of secular celebrations, from funerals to the opening of a new business enterprise. Outside urban areas, monks for centuries provided the only education available to village children, and even today government schools often hold classes within the *wat* precincts. Venerated senior monks attain added status through the widespread sale of tape-recorded sermons and some become nationally known figures. The cremation of one who died recently in the north attracted a crowd numbering more than a million.

Outside the monastery, too, Buddhism makes its presence felt in innumerable subtle ways, often mysterious to the outsider. Such ingrained patterns of Thai social behavior as the avoidance of extremes, acceptance of one's fate, and the emphasis on social harmony above individuality, can all be traced back to Buddhist precepts. For the laity, particularly women, the only hope of advancement in future incarnations lies in the numerous opportunities for making merit, ranging from such simple acts as offering a monk his morning meal to the construction or repair of a *wat*. Nearly every Thai at some time has taken part in a *thot kathin* ceremony, held at the end of the rainy season, in which robes and other necessities are carried to monasteries throughout the

The great 45-meter Reclining Buddha at Bangkok's Wat Po is entirely covered with gold leaf. *Photographer:* **Yow Yun Woh,** Singapore

country by festive groups who combine piety with merrymaking. Some embark annually on such outings, taking robes with them to remote provinces.

Buddhism in Thailand coexists with older beliefs, mostly centering around a host of invisible beings, whose powers are widely believed to extend over many things. In addition to its *wat,* nearly every community also has a shrine that houses its guardian spirit, to whom regular offerings of flowers, incense, and food must be made to ensure prosperity. Cities have these as well. One of the first structures built when Bangkok was founded was Lak Muang, across from the Grand Palace, where homage is paid to the spirit who watches over the fortunes of the capital — and who also, incidentally, has the power to grant wishes of all kinds, from better health to a winning number in the national lottery.

Individual pieces of land have their own spirits, generally provided with shelter in the form of a small house raised on a post and supplied with offerings by the residents. There are spirits, too, of the rice fields, of rivers, of certain trees, of the sea, all of whom must be propitiated in some way.

Thais also rely on other forms of protection for their earthly well-being. Most, for example, wear or carry some kind of amulet, usually in the form of a Buddhist votive plaque, believed to prevent various ills from befalling its owner. Some rely on magic tattoos, frequently of elaborate design, for the same purpose. In addition, astrologers and spiritual mediums are routinely consulted for advice on business matters, personal problems, travel plans, and auspicious dates for nearly every important undertaking.

Tolerance toward other religions has long been a notable characteristic of the kingdom, as evidenced by the variety of beliefs that flourished in 17th-century Ayutthaya. Predominant in the southernmost provinces near the Malaysian border are Muslims, nearly all of them Sunni, who comprise the largest minority group and are given full freedom to practice their faith with support from the King and the government. Christian missionaries came to the country some 400 years ago and have been more or less continuously in residence ever since. Though the number of converts has been small in terms of the total population, Catholics and Protestants have made significant contributions in the fields of education and medicine. Mahayana Buddhists, Hindus, and Sikhs are also present, mainly in urban areas.

Never far beneath the surface of daily life and exerting a pervasive influence over it, Thailand's varied faiths constitute an essential part of its cultural identity. Though separate and distinct, the many paths have come together in the kingdom where they carry on a legacy of tolerance and acceptance.

An ornate temple in Chiang Mai, many of the decorative details on it show Burmese influence.
Photographer: Dominic Sansoni, Sri Lanka

Above: Buddha images at Wat Chiang Man in Chiang Mai.

Right: At Wat Mouwto in the village of Khun Yuan in Mae Hong Son Province, an area in which Thai and Burmese influences intermingle, a priest reads from a sacred text written on a palmleaf manuscript.

Photographer: **Bruno Barbey**, France

Next double page: Monks perform a wide variety of duties in Thai monasteries, ranging from meditation to assorted maintenance chores; some novices also study scriptures during their period in the temple.

Rosine Mazin

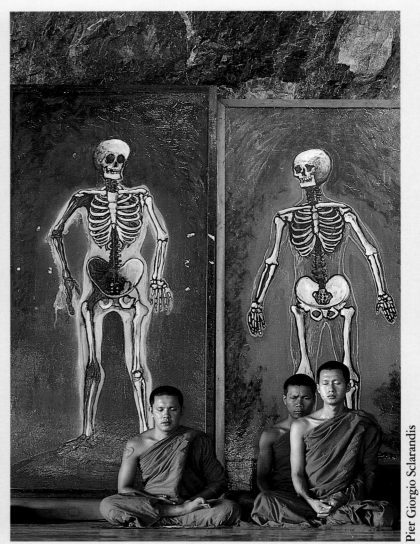

Pier Giorgio Sclarandis

Franco Salmoiraghi

Left: A monk sits before the principal Buddha image in Wat Sri Mongkontai in Mukdahan Province. Other images are also displayed, along with offerings of flowers, candles, and sticks of incense.
Photographer: **George Mitchell,** United States

Above: The Emerald Buddha, first discovered in Chiang Rai in 1434, is the most celebrated image in the kingdom. After being enshrined for centuries at various temples in northern Thailand and Laos, it was brought from Vientiane by the future King Rama I and later made the principal image of his Royal Chapel in Bangkok. It is shown here on its magnificent altar in Wat Phra Keo, in the Grand Palace.
Photographer: **Luca Invernizzi Tettoni,** Italy

Above: Ordination into the Buddhist priesthood,
most commonly during the months of the Rains
Retreat, is one of the basic rites of passage in the
life of a Thai man. The three shown here, from
the village of Lap Lae, are receiving their saffron
robes from a senior monk, while their families
and friends watch.
Photographer: **Michael Freeman,** Great Britain

Below: The presentation of food to monks in the morning is a basic Thai ritual, bringing merit to the person who makes the offering. Here the rite is taking place outside the Marble Temple in Bangkok.
Photographer: **Paul Chesley,** United States

Below (bottom): Monks in a classroom at a temple in Chiang Mai.
Photographer: **Rosine Mazin,** France

One of the more unusual attractions on Koh Samui, an island in the southern part of
the Gulf of Thailand, is an elephant-shaped meditation cell in which pious monks,
like the old man shown here, can escape the world's distractions.
Photographer: **Bernard Hermann,** France

Overleaf: Wat Pai Rong Wou is decorated with realistic paintings of the hell awaiting
Buddhist sinners. The offerings on the stand are a typical assortment: garlands,
incense sticks, fresh flowers, food, and small figurines.
Photographer: **Raghu Rai,** India

Rites of exorcism may be necessary when evil spirits take up residence in the body. The specialist shown here uses various methods to drive an unwanted spirit out, among them water, fire, and a magic rod. If these fail to produce the desired result, he may throw rice, onions, and pieces of charcoal in the face of the victim or, as a last resort, lash him with the spine of a banana leaf.
Photographer: **Jean-Leo Dugast,** France

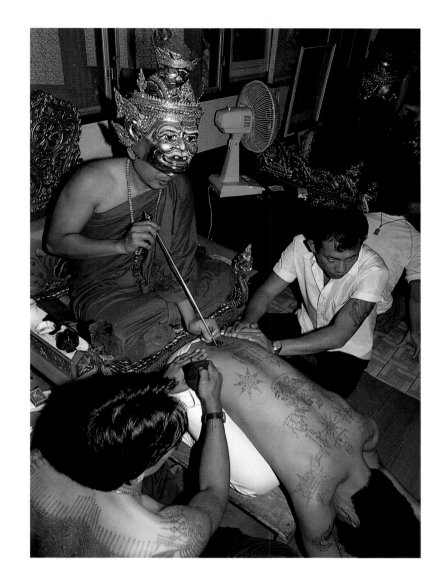

Magical tattoos are no longer as common as they once were, but many Thai men whose livelihood involves risk-taking still believe the arcane designs can protect them from such dangers as bullets and knives. Here some advocates are gathered in the home of a master tattooist in Samut Prakarn, just outside Bangkok. The host, shown above wearing a golden mask, becomes possessed by the spirit of a mythical Hindu ascetic before he applies the tattoos to the back of one of his followers.
Photographer: **Jean-Leo Dugast,** France

Above: A boat-shaped funeral pyre ferries a Buddhist monk to the next life from a field in Chiang Dao in Chiang Mai Province. The rite of cremation is seen as the freeing of the soul. It is a happy occasion because it represents the final destruction of the physical being which has held the soul prisoner.
Photographer: **Dominic Sansoni,** Sri Lanka

Right: Another elaborate cremation ceremony is about to begin at Wat Phuvin in Chiang Rai. The style of the coffin and pavilion vary in different parts of the kingdom. The month of March is traditionally dedicated to funerals and weddings.
Photographer: **Rio Helmi,** Indonesia

The village of Koh Panyi, located in the shadow of a towering limestone rock in Phang Nga Bay, has two separate lives. One is devoted to the tourists who arrive every day to view the picturesque houses on stilts and enjoy the fresh seafood offered by local restaurants. The other, rarely seen by outsiders, is that of a traditional Muslim community which has lived on the island for many years. The women here are shown in the local mosque, the settlement's most prominent structure.
Photographer: **Andris Apse**, New Zealand

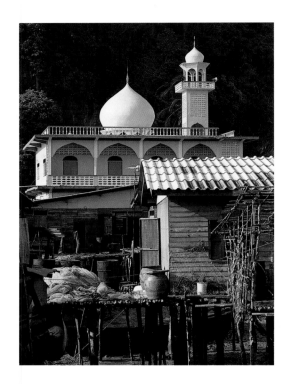

For the Muslim villagers of Koh Panyi, the mosque is the center of their spiritual life. The limestone mountain seen in the picture on the right protects the village from monsoon storms. Koh Panyi itself is also an attraction with its quaint structures built over the water, its towering mosque and its numerous restaurants specializing in fresh seafood caught in the shallow bay. The villagers once derived a livelihood from the manufacture of fish paste but now survive mainly on the tourist trade.
Photographer: **Andris Apse,** New Zealand

Islam is the predominant faith in Thailand's far southern provinces. On the left, a man reads the Koran at the Talok Manok Mosque while, above, Muslim students attend class at the Sanso Pattam High School in Bana, both in Pattani Province.
Photographer: **Abbas,** Iran

Overleaf: Fishermen who derive a living from the seas off Thailand's coasts get their best catches at night with the aid of powerful lights that attract creatures to the surface. This boat off Surat Thani is hauling in nets full of squid.
Photographer: **Pisit Jiropas,** Thailand

Threads in a Traditional Fabric

The overwhelming majority of Thailand's fifty million or so people live in rural areas, mostly in small villages. These differ widely. They may stretch along the bank of a winding river or an arrow-straight canal, lie half hidden under a canopy of trees in the midst of vast rice fields, or perch precariously on stilts over the sea. Their thousand or so inhabitants may earn their livelihood from farming, making handicrafts or fishing. Their homes may reflect affluence or abject poverty. Yet despite their differences, nearly all the country's countless hamlets share certain cultural traits that have been produced and shaped by centuries of tradition.

In most parts of the country the focus of village life outside the immediate family group will be the local *wat,* or Buddhist temple, a much simpler version of those dazzling structures so admired by tourists in Bangkok yet still in marked contrast to the basically modest houses. The *wat* serves a number of religious needs, of course; nearly every young man from the community will spend at least a few months there, usually just before he gets married, the resident monks chant prayers at numerous functions, and maintenance of the *wat* offers opportunities for the vital task of earning personal merit. But it plays a secular role that is equally important. Senior monks are called on to mediate in disputes, meetings are held within its precincts on important local matters, and Buddhist festivals scattered throughout the year are celebrated there.

Left: Homeward bound at sunset on a provincial waterway, one of the timeless scenes of Thai rural life. Despite new roads that now link once-isolated villages, rivers and canals still remain important avenues of communication.
Photographer: **Dominic Sansoni**, Sri Lanka

Photographer (above): **Jean-Leo Dugast**, France

The festivals provide a chance for young people to meet informally and for everyone to forget the hard work that generally characterizes their existence.

Each village is a self-contained unit, governed by an elected head — traditionally a man but sometimes a woman. Its basic rules of personal and social conduct have changed little over the years. Families include not only parents and children but also often grandparents and other relatives, and authority is hierarchical. Children are treated permissively when young but are taught to respect their elders and defer to them in almost everything, a conditioning that is felt throughout their lives. Even if they leave the village, as many from the poorer regions of Thailand do, young people feel a strong sense of responsibility for the welfare of their parents and will continue to send money to support them.

Rural etiquette frowns upon ostentation and displays of emotion. With rare exceptions, the houses are plain wooden structures, raised above the ground to offer protection from floods and also to provide a place to keep the family animals. Little value is placed on privacy, and often several generations live in a single room. Within the family, and in outside society as well, the ideal is what the Thais call a "cool heart," meaning an avoidance of extremes, coupled with a Buddhist acceptance of fate that is reflected in the expression *mai pen rai,* "Never mind, it's all right."

Since agriculture forms the basis of rural economy, village life revolves around the planting cycle. Fields are generally plowed in April or May, just before the advent of the monsoon rains, with rice traditionally the major crop. Despite the introduction of modern machines in some areas, the average farming family will depend on the reliable water buffalo to do this job. Planting is often a communal effort involving the entire community. By the time the rains come, the fields have been planted and there is relatively little to do except watch over the growing rice and ensure that the paddies are supplied with a proper amount of water. It is at this time that many young men enter the priesthood, an essential rite of passage in attaining full maturity. The harvest comes in late November or early December, after which the villagers devote themselves to various other activities — supplementary crops, handicraft production, or perhaps a temporary job in glamorous Bangkok — before the timeless cycle begins again.

Life is not all hard work, however. The Thai penchant for *sanuk,* or fun, finds an outlet even in the smallest hamlet, even in the most solemn rituals. Buddhist celebrations punctuate the year, most calling for a festival of some kind where young and old can gather at the *wat* for pleasure as well as merit-making, and a bountiful crop, auspicious birthdays, or the ordination of a son are also social occasions.

An array of tempting Thai vegetables on display in a typical village marketplace.
Photographer: **G. A. Rossi,** Italy

Limes, chili peppers, spring onions, and ginger root are but a few of the ingredients that are commonly used in Thai cooking.
Photographer: **Dominic Sansoni,** Sri Lanka

There are variations, of course. In the far south, Moslems predominate, and the mosque is as common as the *wat.* Here, moreover, the sea is likely to be the main feature of life and its seasonal moods determine village activity. In the northern mountains, exotic hilltribes lead a largely nomadic existence, clearing farm land by a destructive slash-and-burn technique and planting the lucrative opium poppy for a livelihood. The government is taking steps to curb such activities, however, and the tribal people are increasingly to be found in permanent settlements, cultivating more acceptable crops, such as coffee.

Rural life is not as static as it once was, however. In many parts of the country significant changes are taking place, prompted by a variety of forces that were scarcely known a generation ago.

Over the past several decades, for example, Thailand has built perhaps the most modern network of highways and feeder roads to be found in any Southeast Asian country. Some indication of the magnitude of this achievement can be seen in the fact that the total road system grew from 26,000 kilometers in 1971 to nearly 157,000 kilometers in 1983, meaning that countless once-remote villages are now much more accessible. They can get their produce to urban markets, and at the same time urban influences can reach them in a far shorter time than before. Moreover, while rice is still the basis of rural economy, it has been joined by newer, increasingly important export crops like sugar, tapioca and pineapples. Raw cotton and soya beans are also produced for export and tobacco production is on the rise. Vineyards have been planted and Thai vintners hope to turn out quality wines in due course.

Tourism has transformed other communities, especially along the kingdom's seacoasts. The picturesque little Muslim village of Koh Panyi, in Phang Nga Bay, is now a popular attraction among day-trippers, and most of the fish caught by its residents in the surrounding waters end up in restaurants that cater to these visitors. A much more spectacular metamorphosis has taken place on the Gulf of Thailand at Pattaya, once a sleepy hamlet of a hundred or so fishing families and now perhaps Southeast Asia's best-known seaside resort complex. Busloads of emissaries from the outside world are also bringing wide-ranging social and economic changes elsewhere, particularly in the northern provinces.

Finally, the mass media are breaking down the age-old sense of rural isolation. In 1976, only 19 per cent of Thai villages enjoyed the luxury of electric power; today the inhabitants of over 75 per cent of them can sit before a television set and watch the flickering shapes of the future materialize in their traditional world.

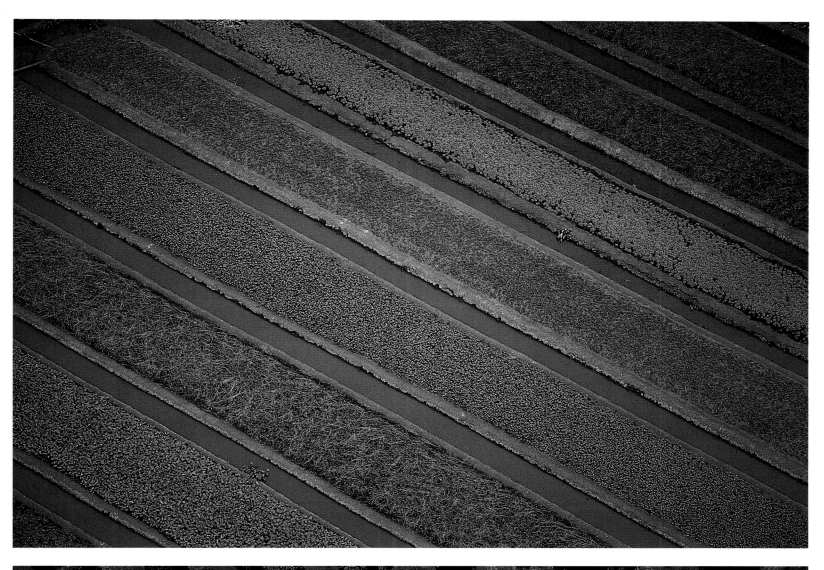

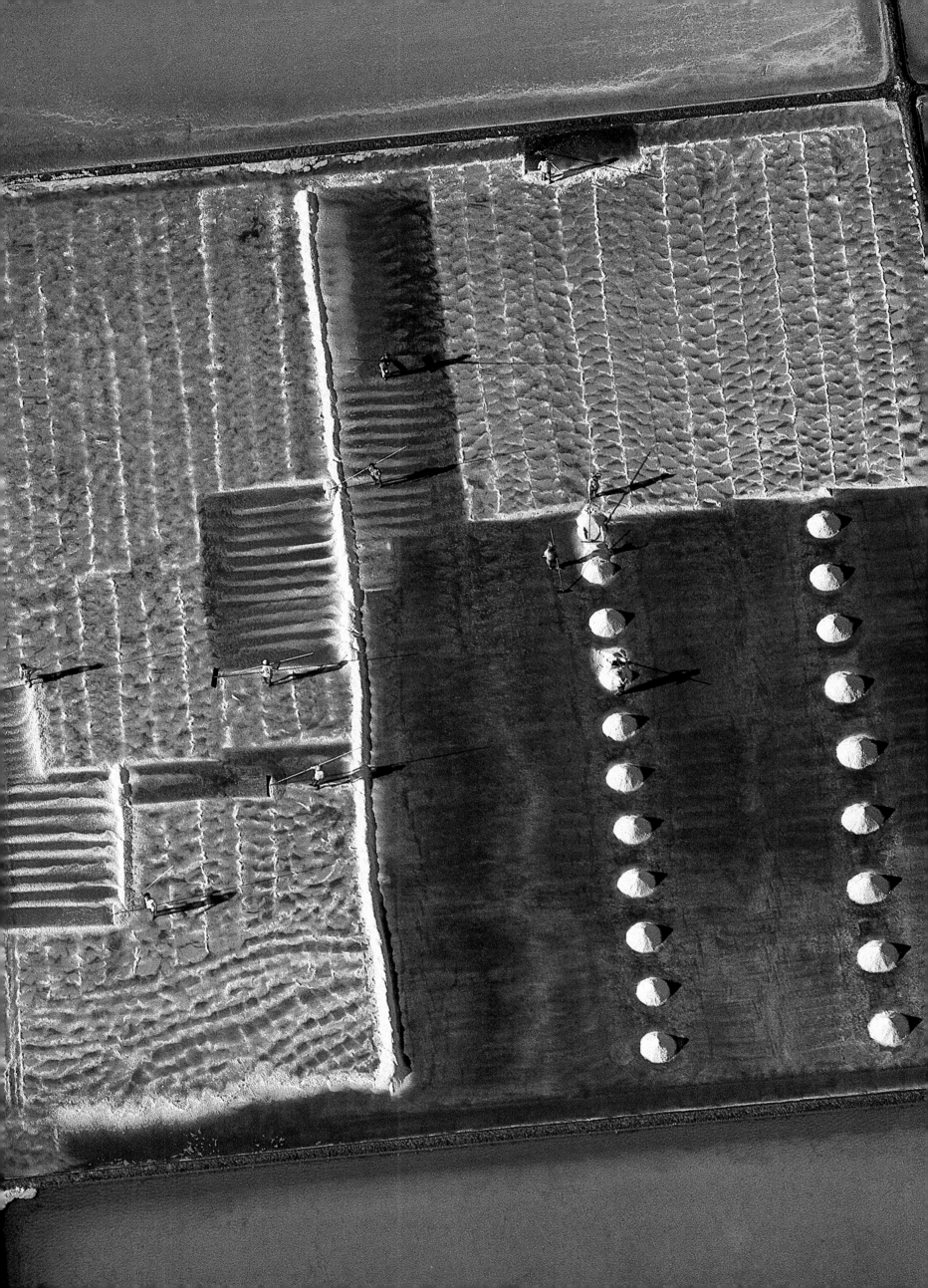

Preceding pages: Rich patterns are revealed in these aerial views from south of Bangkok.
(Left) The fields are being used to produce salt from seawater. *(Right)* Vegetable fields
offer a variety of green hues, while fruit trees thrive in the fertile red earth.
Photographer: **Barrie Rokeach,** United States

Left: An aerial view of salt flats southeast of Bangkok.
Photographer: **Barrie Rokeach,** United States

Above: Laborers at work in the salt flats between Samut Sakhon and Samut Songkhram.
Photographer (top): **Nik Wheeler,** Great Britain
Photographer (bottom): **G.A. Rossi,** Italy

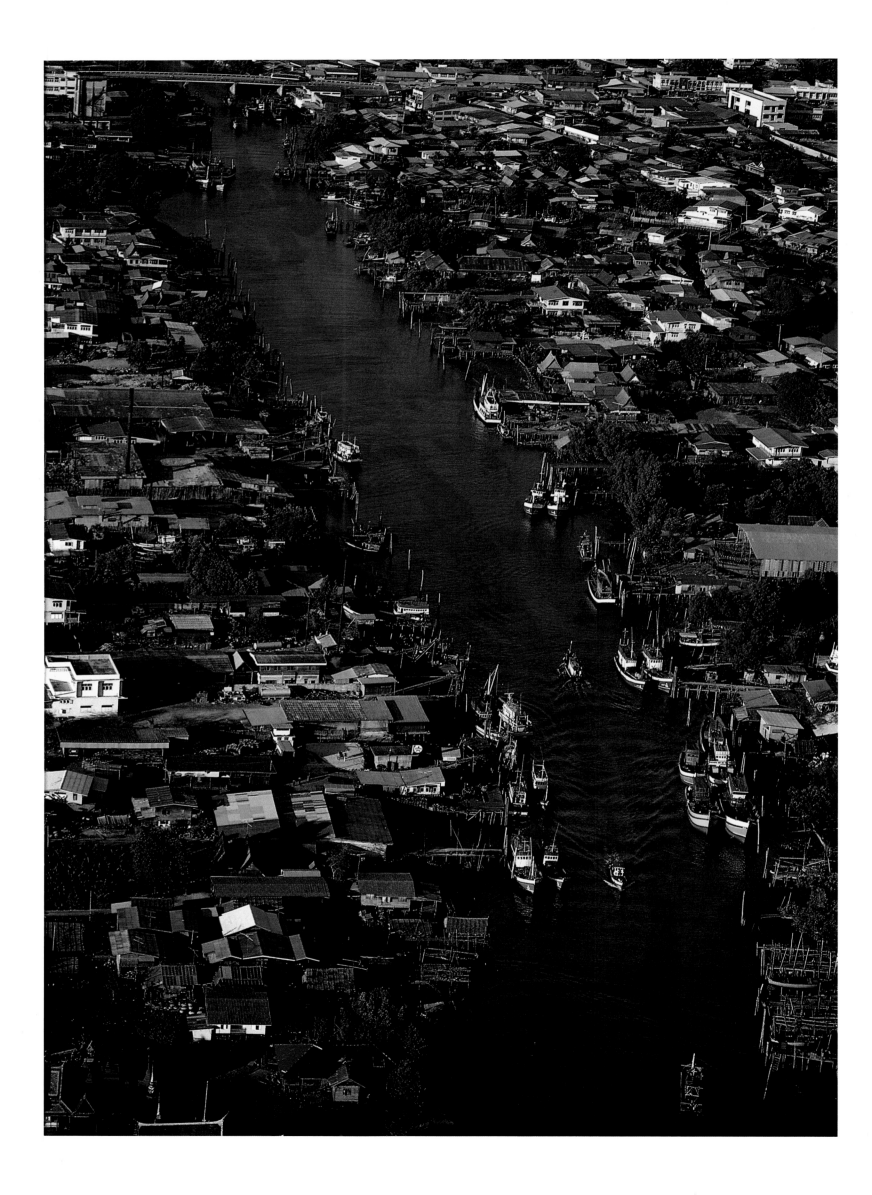

Left: Fishing boats and other craft ply a busy canal southwest of Bangkok, not far from
the rich fishing grounds in the Gulf of Thailand.
Photographer: **Barrie Rokeach,** United States

Above: This wooden bridge on the River Kwai is not the one made famous in the novel
by Pierre Boulle which cost the lives of so many Allied prisoners-of-war during World
War II; it is at a place called Sankhlaburi in Kanchanaburi Province.
Photographer: **Bill Wassman,** United States

Above: Floating markets are still very much a feature of Thai life outside urban areas.
This child is waiting in one of the numerous boats that gather daily at Talad Kon Pitak
on a canal in Nakhon Pathom Province selling everything from fresh vegetables to
household utensils and cooked food.

Right: A girl rests between her market rounds. She sells bowls of freshly cooked
noodles garnished with tasty condiments, perhaps the favorite fast food in Thailand.
Her straw hat provides protection from the sun and also permits air circulation.

Photographer: **Nik Wheeler,** Great Britain

Life in the agricultural village of Lap Lae follows traditional Thai patterns.

Above: Three young men are carried to the village *wat* for their ordination into the
Buddhist monkhood, an occasion that blends solemnity with gaiety.

Right: The top picture shows villagers harvesting spring onions, an alternate crop
grown between rice plantings. In the lower picture, a respected elder resident ties
sacred cords around the wrists of a newly-married couple, thus symbolically binding
them, while their family members watch.
Photographer: **Michael Freeman,** Great Britain

Next double page: In the Ban Peu district of Udon Thani Province, a monk walks past a
curious monument believed to date from prehistoric times. A cell has been created in
the upper part where Buddhist monks in search of solitude can practise meditation.
Photographer: **Bancha Cheunprapanusorn,** Thailand

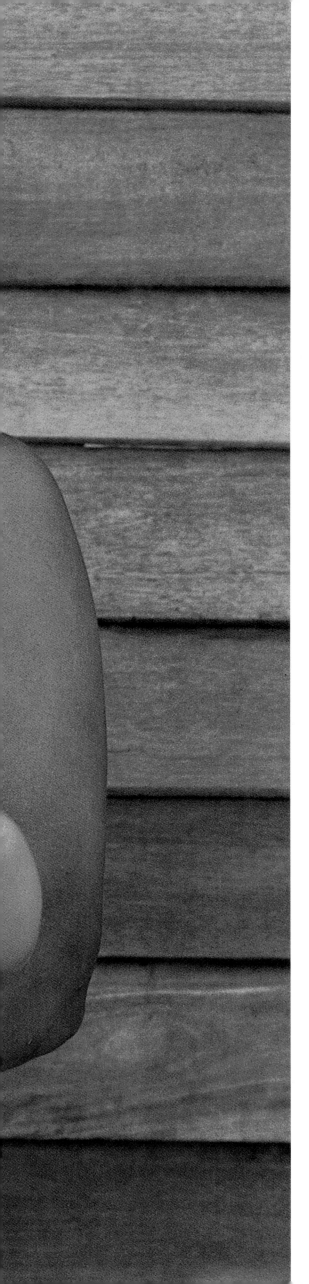

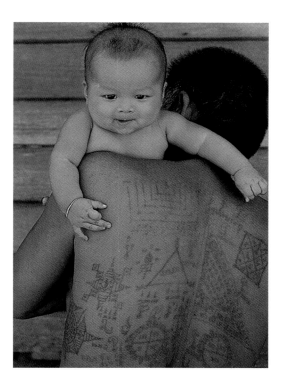

Left and above: A man in Kanchanaburi proudly displays a brace of healthy babies. Like many older people in the provinces, he also displays a variety of tattoos, believed to protect him from numerous dangers.

Photographer: **Joe Carini,** United States

Left: The village of Lap Lae in Uttaradit Province is famous for its pretty girls and its elegantly-made brooms, both of which are shown here.
Photographer: **Michael Freeman,** Great Britain

Above: A fisherman works on his nets at Songkhla before going out into the Gulf of Thailand. While fishing as a means to earn a livelihood is on the decline, deep-sea fishing for sport is gaining in popularity.
Photographer: **Franco Salmoiraghi,** United States

Above: Along Thailand's three coasts — two on the Gulf and one of the Indian Ocean — the sea dominates the life of many people, yielding a variety of riches. Here, on a beach in the Cheang Thong Islands off Surat Thani Province, a woman uses a net stretched in the sun to dry squid, a popular snack throughout much of the kingdom.
Photographer: **Pisit Jiropas,** Thailand

Right: Off Koh Samui, in the southern part of the Gulf of Thailand, an employee of the Naga Pearl Farm performs a delicate operation to insert "seeds" in oysters. These oysters will then be placed in baskets and lowered into the sea while the pearls are formed. The Japanese introduced this process into Thailand and now there are several pearl farms, most of them operated as joint ventures; what was reportedly one of the largest cultured pearls ever found in the world came from this farm.
Photographer: **Bernard Hermann,** France

Left: The pristine beaches of Koh Samui are attracting numbers of Western travelers, like this girl inspecting the goods of a vendor on Lamai Beach. The demon statue below, of Hindu origin, provides an arresting surprise for strollers along the beach.
Photgrapher: **Bernard Hermann**, France

Above: This fishing boat near the village of Ban Nathon creates the sort of picturesque scene that will undoubtedly lead to increased tourist development on the island of Koh Samui, which so far is accessible only by ferry boat from Surat Thani on the Thai mainland.
Photographer: **Bernard Hermann,** France

Overleaf: Water buffalos take a cooling dip along the river in Ayutthaya Province, in the heart of Thailand's greatest rice-producing region. Though modern agricultural machinery is being used, most Thai farmers still rely on the strong family buffalo to plow their fields.
Photographer: **Steve Vidler,** Great Britain

Steve Vidler

Coconut plantations are one of the most characteristic sights in southern Thailand,
with the nuts being used for food and also copra production. These scenes are from
Koh Samui in the Gulf of Thailand, an island almost entirely covered with the palms.
It is said that the coconuts here are the best in Thailand.
Photographer: **Bernard Hermann**, France

Above: A star student at the Monkey Training School in Surat Thani poses with two of his learning aids. By the end of the course offered by the school, the monkeys are able to scale a lofty coconut palm, select ripe nuts, and throw them down to a keeper waiting below. Most of the large coconut plantations in southern Thailand employ this method of harvesting.
Photographer: **Pisit Jiropas,** Thailand

Left: Thailand is currently the world's third largest producer of natural rubber, most of which comes from plantations in the south. Because the light is dim in the thick forests, many tappers like these at the Nathawee Rubber Plantation on Phuket use headlamps as they go about their work. Rubber trees were introduced to the island in 1903.
Photographer: **Nicholas DeVore,** United States

Above (top): This young elephant knows where to go for a snack in a Surin Province village. The annual "Elephant Roundup" has become a popular tourist attraction.
Photographer: **John Everingham,** Australia

Above: Elephants provide entertainment for visitors at Pattaya, Thailand's leading seaside resort southeast of Bangkok.
Photographer: **Hyacinthe Cao,** Tahiti

Right: Two mother elephants keep a watchful eye on their young at the Elephant Training School in Lampang, the only one of its kind in the kingdom.
Photographer: **John Everingham,** Australia

Chokchai Bulakul is an important figure in the development of the northeast, a region
plagued by poor soil and frequent droughts. On his ranch in Nakhon Ratchasima
Province, he has horses and what is reportedly the largest herd of dairy cows in Asia.
He also keeps some more unusual animals, like a pair of tigers raised from babyhood.
Photographer: **Tom Chuawiwat**, Thailand

In the 1920s railways linked Bangkok with Chiang Mai, in the north, and the Malaysian border in the far south, bringing those regions more closely under the control of the central government. Despite the rapid growth of inter-provincial buses, train travel is still popular with a large segment of the population.

Left: Passengers settle down on the Southern Express for the long trip from Bangkok to Hat Yai, the main railway terminus in the far south.
Photographer: **Joe Carini,** United States

Above (left): At Nakhon Pathom, southwest of Bangkok, vendors gather at the train station to sell fish and prawns to passengers.
Photographer: **Nik Wheeler,** Great Britain

Above (right): Railway employees at the Makkasan Station in Bangkok; many tracks still pass through the heart of the busy capital.
Photographer: **Joe Carini,** United States

Above: New highways have opened many formerly remote regions. These street scenes were taken in the rapidly-growing northeastern city of Nakhon Phanom on the bank of the Mekong River. The leisurely pedicab coexists in such places along with more contemporary forms of public transportation such as the crowded minibus.
Photographer: **George Mitchell,** United States

Right: Morning traffic begins to fill the streets of Phetchaburi, a city south of Bangkok that is rich in ancient remains. Wat Mahatat, a former Khmer temple dating from the 12th century, looms over the modern scene.
Photographer: **Mark Howard,** Great Britain

The Thai love of bright colors finds many outlets in assorted pop arts, among them the adornment of vehicles, especially trucks and motorized tricycles. In addition to abstract designs and lashings of chromium, portraits of folk heroes and movie stars in the style of Andy Warhol are popular. The faces most in demand are macho types like Al Pacino, Robert Redford, and rugged Clint Eastwood.
Photographer: **Mike Hosken**, New Zealand

A group of northeasterners in Mukdahan
Province participate in the *Bai Sri* ceremony,
which celebrates a special occasion such as the
arrival or departure of a distinguished guest.
Photographer: **Bancha Cheunprapanusorn,**
Thailand

Next double page: These huts dot a lake in the
northern province of Mae Hong Son. Local
fishermen use them to escape the heat of the day
while fishing for their family's dinner.
Photographer: **Bruno Barbey,** France

A Lahu village in Mae Hong Son Province. The Lahu, like most of the tribal groups, have their own distinctive dress, with red predominating in the costumes of the women.
Photographer: **Bruno Barbey,** France

Left: A Lisu girl in Mae Hong Son Province wears her tribal finery. In 1983, some 18,000 Lisu were living in 110 villages in Thailand; other groups are found in China, Burma, and in the northeast of India. Lisu clothing is among the brightest of all the tribal groups, their silver jewelry among the most abundant.

Above: This child is a Black Lahu, one of the two main sub-divisions of the Lahu tribal group, the other being the Yellow Lahu.

Photographer: **Bruno Barbey,** France

Above: Members of the Akha hilltribe in the village of Sanchai gather for their evening meal. The Akha, who numbered about 24,000 in 1983, originally migrated from the southern Chinese province of Yunnan. They live in villages readily identifiable by the massive thatched roofs of their houses and a towering swing used in local ceremonies.

Right: An Akha girl displaying the elaborate finery of her dress. The helmet-like headdress is adorned with silver buttons, coins and beads, and the indigo-blue jacket is richly embroidered. Akha girls begin spinning cloth when they are six or seven years old and later take great pains with their costumes.

Photographer: **Leong Ka Tai,** Hong Kong

Among the tribal people living in Thailand's
far north is one comparatively small group that
calls itself the "yellow leaf people" or Hua Yua.
Nomadic by tradition, they move to a new
locality whenever the leaves with which they
make their shelter-homes turn yellow. Those
shown on these pictures were photographed in
Nan Province where the Thai border
meets those of Laos and Burma.
Photographer: **Rio Helmi,** Indonesia

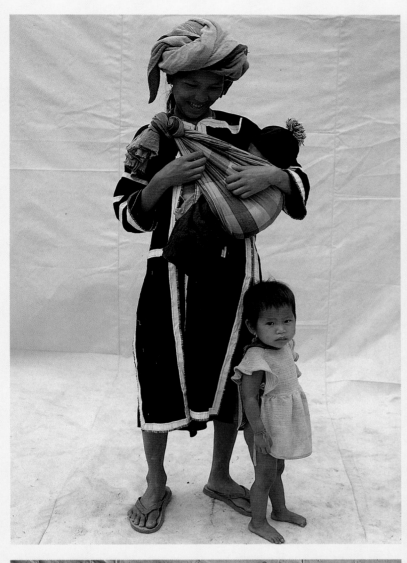

Preceding pages: Among the northerners in this collection of portraits are a pair of policemen from Mae Sot on the Burmese border, some farmers, and a sampling of spectacularly-clad members of the various tribal groups who live in the region.
Photographer: **Patrick Gauvain,** Great Britain

A mobile studio was set up daily in various locations near the Burmese border. A
cheroot-smoking lowland farmer stands proudly between his two wives in the picture
on the left, while a family of Yao strike a pose in their distinctive costume.
Photographer: **Patrick Gauvain**, Great Britain

Color plays an important part in the lives of the hilltribes of Thailand's far north, as seen in the magnificently attired girls above and even in the more prosaic garments worn by the school children on the right.
Photographer: **Patrick Gauvain**, Great Britain

Overleaf: An aerial view of a beach near Pattaya, Thailand's best-known beach resort,
offering a wide range of water sports to residents of Bangkok, only two hours' ride
away, as well as to tourists from all over the world.
Photographer: **Barrie Rokeach,** United States

Barrie Rokeach

Left: Pattaya, on the east coast of the Gulf of Thailand, has become one of the major resorts in the region over the past two decades. This has led to the development of such attractions as Pattaya Park with its slides.
Photographer: **Barrie Rokeach,** United States

Above: Phuket, already one of Thailand's wealthiest provinces because of its rich tin deposits and rubber plantations, offers pellucid waters and idyllic scenes such as those found at Nai Harn Bay and the newly opened Club Med village at Kata Beach.
Photographer (top): **Nicholas DeVore,** United States
Photographer (bottom): **Alberto Cassio,** Italy

Club Méditerranée opened a branch on Phuket in
1985, offering its popular mixture of
entertainment and relaxation. Above is shown one
of the nightly stage shows provided for guests by
the club's staff, while on the top right is the
swimming pool overlooking Kata Bay.
Photographer: **Alberto Cassio,** Italy

Right: Young honeymooners enjoy a cool drink behind an artificial waterfall at the Phuket Yacht Club, a luxury hotel that opened on Nai Harn Beach in 1986. Today there are hotels on nearly all of Phuket's splendid beaches and an international airport to lure foreign travelers.
Photographer: **Nicholas DeVore**, United States

Franco Salmoiraghi

Preceding pages: Rich deposits of oil and natural gas were discovered in the Gulf of Thailand toward the end of the 1970s, easing the kingdom's energy problems and giving rise to new industrial complexes. The Union Oil rig shown here is located in the Erawan oil field off the coast at Songkhla.

Photographer: **Franco Salmoiraghi**, United States

Above: Modern industry is making an
appearance in a number of parts of the country.
This is a gas-separation plant on the east coast
of the Gulf of Thailand, where natural gas and
oil have been discovered in large quantities.
The Eastern Seaboard Project, part of the Fifth
Five-Year Plan comprises the gas-separation
facility, a fertilizer plant, a petrochemical
complex, and a soda-ash plant.
Photographer: **Joe Brignolo,** United States

Far left and below: Metal is smelted in Saraburi
Province at the Siam Iron and Steel Company,
part of the Siam Cement Company Group.
Photographer: **Yow Yun Woh,** Singapore

Above: A pipe rack and crude oil metering station on the Gulf of Thailand is part of the vast Eastern Seaboard Project spawned by the discovery of oil in the Gulf.
Photographer: **Joe Brignolo,** United States

Right: A worker in the southern province of Nakhon Si Thammarat.
Photographer: **Pier Giorgio Sclarandis,** Italy

Next double page: Against a peerless backdrop formed by the spires of the Grand Palace and the Temple of the Emerald Buddha, Sanam Luang, the "Royal Field", is crowded with kite flyers in the late afternoon.
Photographer: **Paul Chesley,** United States

$\mathcal{A}$ Multi-faceted Urban Mosaic

*T*hailand's capital — known internationally as Bangkok but to Thais as Krung Thep, or City of Angels — sprawls over an area of some 1,500 square kilometers on both sides of the Chao Phya River. A complex, constantly changing metropolis it is not merely forty-five times the size of its nearest rival but also the kingdom's unchallenged cultural, commercial, and political center — the exemplar of modern urban life.

Here the King has his official residence and presides over the magnificent ceremonies that have traditionally symbolized the Thai monarchy. Here are located all the government ministries, the military and police headquarters, the Supreme Patriarchate of the Buddhist faith, the most prestigious universities and preparatory schools, the leading banks and business firms, the best medical facilities, the greatest collections of art, the newspaper publishers, the studios that produce films for movie and television screens across the nation. And here, too can be found the most varied collection of Thais from all parts of the kingdom and foreigners, some six or seven million by the latest rough estimate, drawn by the magnetic allure of Bangkok's dynamic tempo and limitless possibilities.

Established as the capital by King Rama I, founder of the Chakri Dynasty, it was originally a water-oriented city modeled after the splendid Ayutthaya further upriver.

Left: One writer has described driving in Bangkok
as creative; others, perhaps in the majority, regard
it as nightmarish. Whatever position one takes,
the city's dense traffic is among its most
memorable features to visitors.
Photographer: **Hiroshi Suga**, Japan

Photographer (above): **Raghu Rai**, India

Like Ayutthaya, it was centered on an artificial island, with a network of canals serving as the principal thoroughfares, and many of the first buildings were obviously aimed at evoking the old capital, which had ruled the kingdom for 400 years before the destruction by the Burmese. This early aspiration is still vividly apparent in the dazzling mile-square Grand Palace enclosure, where golden spires and swooping multi-tiered roofs constitute one of the world's great architectural attractions. More evidence can be found at a number of neighboring temples that are lavishly adorned with the finest of classical Thai arts.

Elsewhere in the same general area can be seen the broad avenues, ornate bridges, and stately Romanesque buildings that reflect royal dreams of a later generation, this time of investing Bangkok with the grandeur of a European capital along the orderly lines of Paris or Berlin. By then, though, it was already too late: even in its early days, Bangkok had displayed a stubborn resistance to sensible city planning, a tendency to expand with a wayward momentum of its own in often unpredictable directions, and this was to prove one of its most enduring characteristics.

Growing trade fueled the rise of a prosperous commercial class, concentrated for over a century in the ghetto-like world of Yaowaraj, or Chinatown, and then spilling out in all directions like the flood waters that periodically inundated the city. Once-vital canals, even the great Chao Phya itself, became increasingly irrelevant as roads stretched across former swamps and rice fields, far from Rama I's palace, bringing with them new centers of population and power and, ultimately, a new Bangkok dependent now upon expressways not waterways.

Yaowaraj continues to exert a distinctive atmosphere with its noisy, narrow alleyways, gleaming displays of gold chains, and bold red banners emblazoned with Chinese characters. It bustles with commerce by day and night, but the really high-powered business deals are made over in a newer financial center along Silom Road, a district of lofty white skyscrapers where state-of-the-art computers hum and bankers negotiate complex transactions in offices high above the traffic-clogged streets. Though crowds still flock to the legendary Weekend Market, browsing through canvas-covered stalls that offer everything from housewares and herbal medicines to fruits and fuchsia-colored Siamese fighting fish, others — especially the young, who comprise the majority of Bangkok's present population — are more likely to prefer one of the vast, air-conditioned shopping centers that have mushroomed throughout the city. In the space of a single decade, gleaming high-rise buildings have created a dramatic new skyline in central areas, dwarfing the drab rows of shophouses.

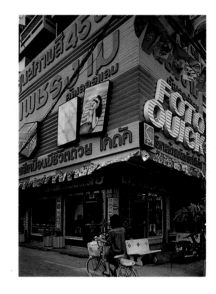

A photography shop adds color to a typical Bangkok street, with signs that disguise an otherwise mundane row house.
Photographer: **Nik Wheeler,** Great Britain

Most of the three million tourists who come to Thailand each year arrive at Don Muang International Airport, a hub of air travel in Southeast Asia serving some thirty airlines. The airport has just undergone extensive expansion and renovation, making it one of the region's best. Tourists spend the major part of their stay in one of Bangkok's numerous hotels. With nightfall, the city's highly varied entertainment world comes to life, a seductive blend of the *louche* and the luxurious that appeals to locals and visitors alike and enjoys an international reputation of its own.

Here and there, vestiges of a more leisurely lifestyle linger: turreted Victorian villas overlooking the timeless river, commodious bungalows set in shady gardens, even a few surviving canals arched by venerable raintrees, where the din of traffic is replaced by the occasional roar of a long-tailed motorboat. For most city residents, though, home is more likely to be the upper floors of a row shop, a town house, or one of the countless housing estates that have sprung up in the suburbs in sometimes striking styles of architecture — Swiss chalet, mock-Tudor and what one builder calls Thai Gothic.

At least for the present, Bangkok is also the center of an industrial revolution that is gradually moving the Thai economy away from its traditional agrarian base. Modern factories on the city's outskirts are turning out a wide range of export products, among them textiles, wearing apparel, integrated circuits, processed foods, and chemical products. Most reach the outside world via the Port of Bangkok at Klong Toey, which handles around 5.1 million metric tons of cargo annually.

Life in the capital may be the ultimate in Thai urban living, but new urban centers have emerged in the provinces and several old ones have been revitalized by tourism, industry, and a vastly improved system of inter-provincial transportation and communication, which continues to expand.

Nakhon Ratchasima in the northeast, for example, is now second only to Bangkok in population. Chiang Mai, one of the oldest provincial capitals, not only continues to serve as the principal coordination point for northern agriculture but has also become a major tourist destination, with an international airport and a big-city bustle replacing its once-bucolic pace. The discovery of oil and natural gas in the Gulf of Thailand has brought new-found prosperity and increased urbanization to the eastern seaboard. Southern cities like Surat Thani, Phuket, and Hat Yai, long isolated by distance and insufficient transportation, have acquired increasing importance in recent years as well as many of Bangkok's modern ways.

Both metaphorically and literally, all roads may still lead to Bangkok, but today there are more than a few stops along the way for those in search of bright lights.

Fast foods have caught on in the city, especially with the younger set; McDonalds now has several outlets.
Photographer: **Leonard Lueras,** United States

Overleaf: An aerial view of Bangkok City; in the center of the picture can be seen the gilded spires of the Grand Palace sited on the banks of the Chao Phya River.
Photographer: **Barrie Rokeach,** United States

Barrie Rokeach

The broad Chao Phya River remains an important artery of communication in Bangkok. On the left, river taxis carry commuters home at the end of the day while, above, the 86-meter *prang* of Wat Arun (the Temple of Dawn), one of the capital's premier attractions, towers over some lesser craft.
Photographer: **Yow Yun Woh**, Singapore

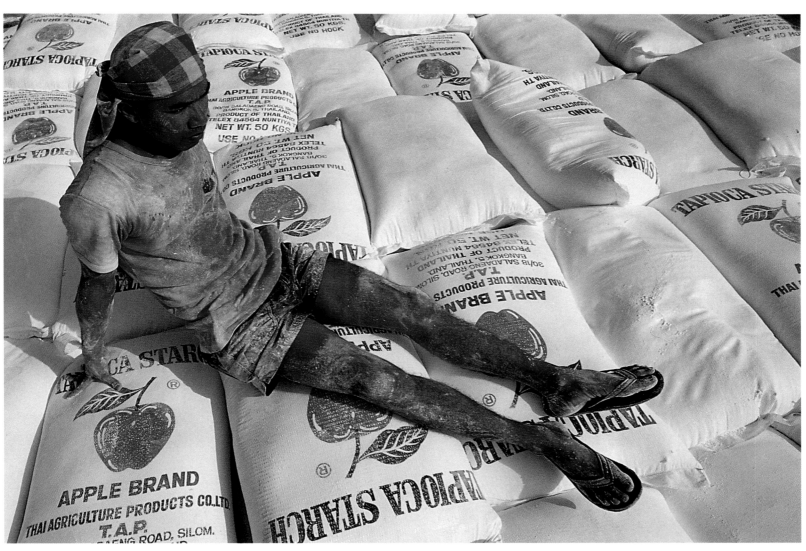

Preceding pages: Some people claim the long-tail motorboat originated in Thailand. The propeller extending from the rear can be raised or lowered, making it possible for the boats to be used in shallow canals and rice fields as well as deeper waters.
Photographer: **Paul Chesley,** United States

Cassava, the plant from which tapioca is made, is one of Thailand's major crops, and the kingdom now ranks as the world's leading exporter. Tapioca flour is used industrially, as well as for the making of chips and pellets in animal feed. The workers shown on these pages are loading sacks of flour on barges at a Union Godown.
Photographer: **Paul Chesley,** United States

Left: Chinatown is one of Bangkok's oldest districts, originally settled by a group of traders who lived on the site selected for the Grand Palace. While it is no longer the main business center, it continues to preserve its distinctive atmosphere. Here a resident prepares food in her kitchen in the crowded quarter.

Above: Customs in the district remain purely Chinese for the most part. Here some traditional offerings are on display at the funeral of a woman, whose picture is exhibited before her coffin. Among them are dishes of food, elaborate floral wreaths, and paper figures that will be burned during the ceremony.

Photographer: **Wang Miao,** China

Above: Gold shops abound in Yaowaraj, Bangkok's Chinatown, attracting buyers from all over the capital. Besides jewelry like the pieces on display here, the shops sell gold chains in different weights, preferred by many Thais as an easily portable means of investment. *Photographer:* **Wang Miao,** China

Below: A typical street scene in Yaowaraj shows how the Chinese influence is more conspicious in this district than in other parts of the city, with Chinese signs as common as Thai ones.
Photographer: **Wang Miao,** China

Below (bottom): Incense sticks, used in countless ceremonies, come in a wide range of sizes. Workers are applying red dye to these huge specimens at a Bangkok factory.
Photographer: **Jean-Leo Dugast,** France

Street vendors of all kinds are a traditional part of the Bangkok scene, despite repeated efforts by authorities to banish them to fixed market areas. This girl vendor has all the ingredients for a quickly-assembled salad, all prepared. These are popular with busy housewives. The shops behind her sell inexpensive clothing and other goods.
Photographer: **Paul Montri**, Thailand

Curbside snacking is a favorite Bangkok leisure activity *(top)*, and thousands of
sidewalk restaurants cater to the demand all over the city. The man is selling garlands
composed mostly of strongly scented jasmine, strung by hand into intricate coronals.
These garlands are used as offerings at shrines.
Photographer: **Paul Montri,** Thailand

Left: A Bangkok photography studio displays a selection of portraits of illustrious subjects, most of them prominent military figures in full-dress uniform.
Photographer: **Gerald Gay,** Singapore

Above (top): This studio, also in Bangkok, appears to specialize in pictures of children.
Photographer: **Gerald Gay,** Singapore

Above: Graduation pictures are proof of academic attainments and hang in many Thai homes for proud parents to enjoy.
Photographer: **Steve Vidler,** Great Britain

In March, a dependable late-afternoon breeze not only comes as welcome relief from the heat of the day but also signals the start of the kite-flying season. Crowds gather for the sport at Bangkok's Sanam Luang, the large oval field across from the Grand Palace, among them the enthusiastic children on the left and the pair of identical twins below. Adults, too, participate in the activity by staging epic sky battles between huge "male" kites, each requiring a team of up to ten men, and smaller but more maneuverable "females," the object being to see which can bring the other to the ground.
Photographer: **Gerald Gay,** Singapore

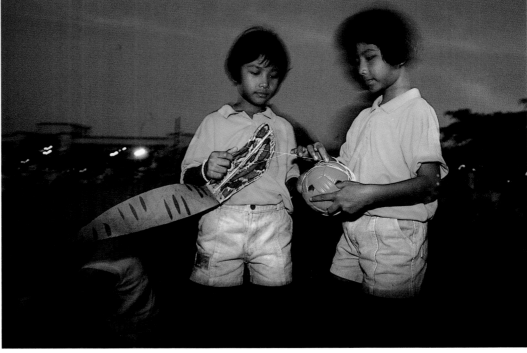

Horse-racing is a Western sport that has found widespread appeal among Thais, especially in the capital, which has two tracks. The horses shown here at the Royal Bangkok Sports Club are smaller than their Western counterparts and are specially bred to stand up under the demands of a tropical climate.
Photographer: **G.A. Rossi**, Italy

Golf made its debut in Thailand in the 1920s and has become a sport popular among affluent Thais all over the kingdom. As in the West, many business deals are struck on these golf courses. The pictures above show the caddies at the Rose Garden, a resort an hour's drive from Bangkok, stylishly attired in their distinctive uniforms.
Photographer: **G.A. Rossi**, Italy

Left: Takraw, a popular sport which involves keeping a woven rattan ball aloft by means of feet, knees, thighs, chest, shoulders and head, is capable of many variations. These boys play near the ruins of Ayutthaya.
Photographer: **John Everingham**, Australia

Below: An indoor takraw game, being played at the PATA Department Store in Bangkok.
Photographer: **G. A. Rossi**, Italy

Below (bottom): A Thai boxer delivers a swift left kick that is as lethal as it is graceful.
Photographer: **G. A. Rossi**, Italy

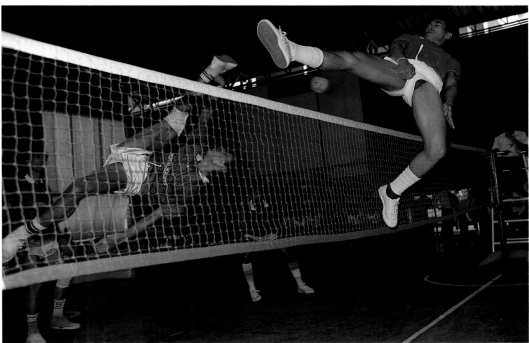

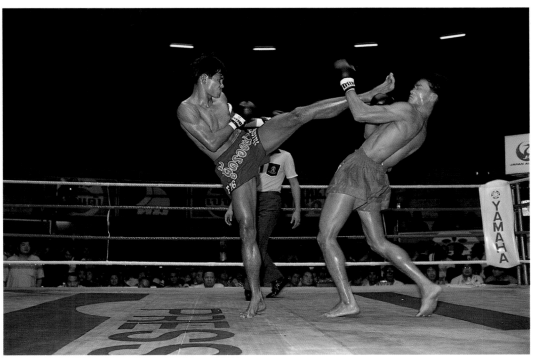

Khun Preecha Sowanna, who has won the bodybuilding title "Mr. Thailand" six
times, strikes a few poses to demonstrate how he won the title during a workout at the
Bangkok Hilton Hotel's Clark Hatch Fitness Center.
Photographer: **Leonard Lueras,** United States

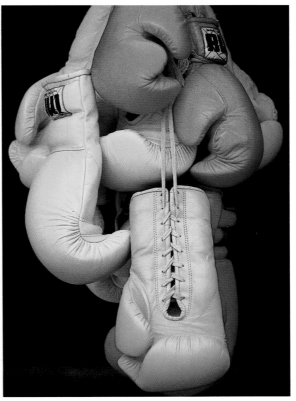

Thai boxers undergo a rigorous training program to get them into shape for the ring and
the trophies they hope to win. Shown here are some of the fighters under Khun Chanai,
coach of the Thai national team and trainer of numerous champions.
Photographer: **G.A. Rossi,** Italy

Above (top): Sixty per cent of Thailand's population is under 19 years of age, making education one of the kingdom's major current concerns. These lively uniformed school children are waiting with one of their teachers in front of Bangkok's Wat Phra Keo.
Photographer: **Gerald Gay**, Singapore

Above: A young girl ponders a lesson at one of Thailand's largest orphanages, located in Wat Sri Gaen in Angthong Province, near the old capital of Ayutthaya.
Photographer: **Steve Vidler**, Great Britain

Right: Two Girl Guides enjoy a soft drink after their extra-curriculum activities.
Photographer: **Paul Chesley**, United States

Above and right (top): Growing up in Bangkok's huge Klong Toey slum, near the capital's port, gave young Prateep Ungsongtham firsthand knowledge of its people's needs. She later established the Pattana Village Community School in the heart of the slum and has won widespread recognition for her achievements, including the 1978 Magsaysay Award for Public Service. Slum children are shown here.
Photographer: **Koes,** Indonesia

Right: The Satit Chula Demonstration School, run by the prestigious Chulalongkorn University, is regarded as one of the best in Bangkok, with strict entrance requirements. These children are enjoying themselves during a recess from class.
Photographer: **Melinda Berge,** United States

Students at Vajiravudh College in Bangkok wear uniforms reminiscent of official dress during the reign of the sixth Chakri King, who established the school and whose statue stands outside one of its ornate buildings. The college is one of the top-ranking preparatory schools and most of its graduates go on to study at a prominent university.
Photographer: **Koes,** Indonesia

Above (top): A student reviews her notes between classes at Chulalongkorn University, Thailand's oldest and most prestigious institution of higher learning.
Photographer: **Melinda Berge**, United States

Above: The Asian Institute of Technology, a unique post-graduate institution, is located some 40 kilometers north of Bangkok. Students from nearly 20 Asian countries specialize in a wide range of subjects taught by Western and Asian technical experts.
Photographer: **Koes**, Indonesia

Right: Students sing the National Anthem at the Assumption Convent in Bangkok. The first schools for girls were founded by missionaries in the 19th century.
Photographer: **Paul Chesley**, United States

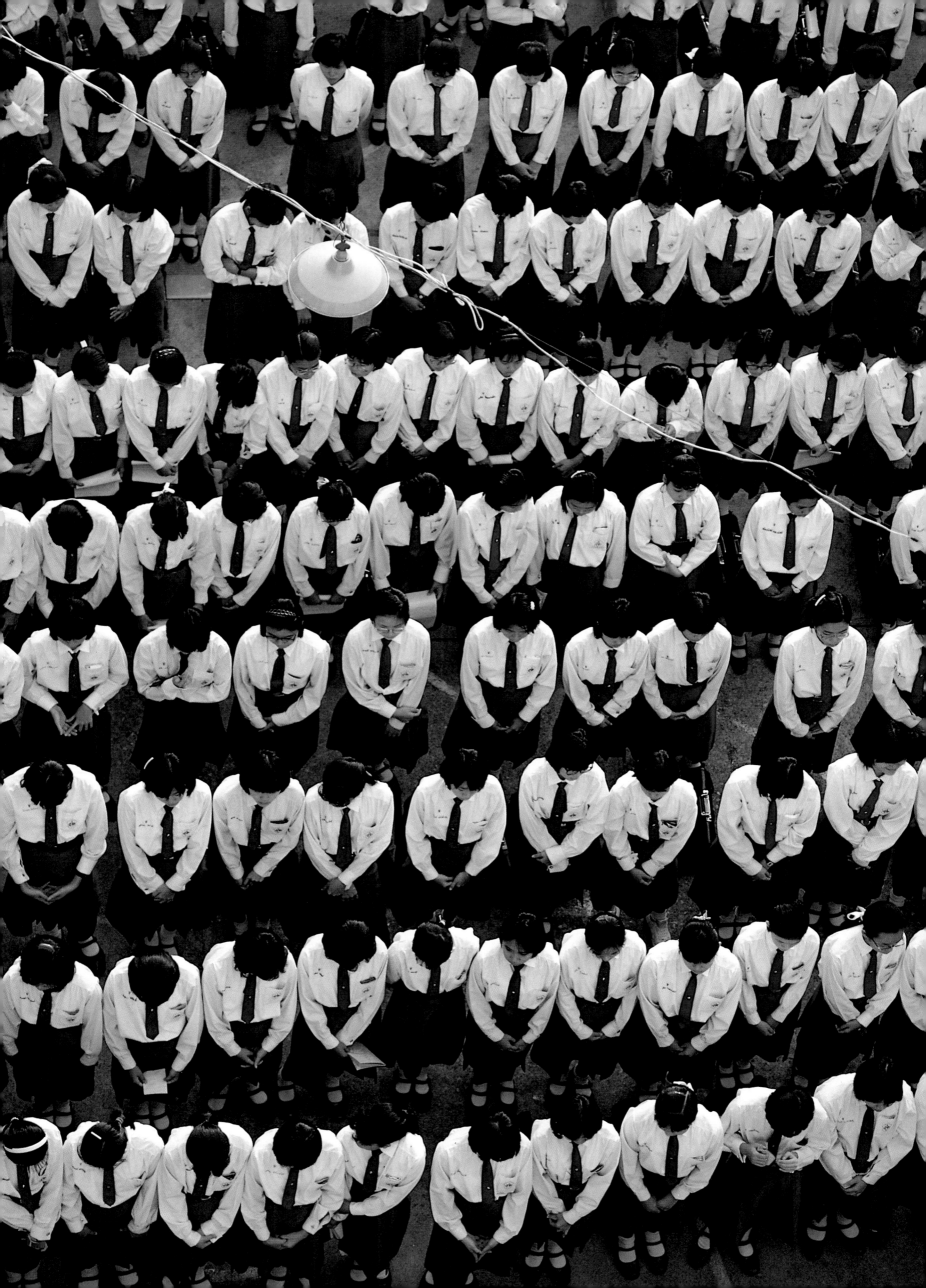

One of the more unusual museums in Bangkok, Siriraj Hospital, is devoted to exhibits related to forensic medicine. These boys are fascinated by the preserved body of a notorious murderer named Si Quey, who killed children and ate their livers. Thai mothers used to frighten recalcitrant offspring by threatening to call upon his services.
Photographer: **Yow Yun Woh,** Singapore

In another Siriraj Hospital museum, a medical student takes notes on a pair of
conjoined twins, usually known in the West as Siamese twins. The famous originals
were first spotted in 1824 by an English resident of Bangkok. The twins were
swimming in the Chao Phya River not far from where the hospital is presently located.
Photographer: **Yow Yun Woh**, Singapore

Paul Chesley

Preceding pages: Under the watch of two armed
guards, employees of the Bangkok Bank Ltd.
count packets of 500-baht notes in the bank's
skyscraper headquarters in the capital. The
Bangkok Bank Ltd. is the largest of Thailand's
private financial institutions.
Photographer: **Paul Chesley,** United States

Since its founding in 1960, Thai Airways International has enjoyed a remarkable success. The national carrier had the first all-jet fleet of any regional airline and pioneered jet service to once-remote destinations as Bali and Nepal.

Left: A trio of aircraft awaits unloading and maintenance at Bangkok's Don Muang International airport.

Above: A flight crew waves *Sawasdee* prior to their departure while the picture below shows mechanics inspecting a jet engine in Don Muang's maintenance facility.

Photographer: **Luca Invernizzi Tettoni,** Italy

Above: Lavish wedding receptions, usually held at one of Bangkok's large hotels, are an important part of the social scene. This one, at the Hyatt Central Plaza Hotel, was the reception of Mr. Diloklab Tantriyanond and Miss Samaporn Sivapirunthap.
Photographer: **Melinda Berge,** United States

Right: M.R. Kukrit Pramoj is often described as Thailand's Renaissance man. A former Prime Minister, he has also been a leading novelist (his *Four Reigns* is a panoramic view of Thai society over half a century), journalist (he founded the highly respected newspaper *Siam Rath,* in which he writes a column), movie actor (he appeared opposite Marlon Brando in *The Ugly American*), economist, and noted exponent of Thai classical dance. He is shown here in his Thai-style house which is filled with antiques including masks used in classical dance.
Photographer: **Raghu Rai,** India

Below: One of the last of Bangkok's royally sponsored monasteries, the Wat Benchamabohphit is usually called the Marble Temple because its walls feature white Carrara marble imported by King Rama V in 1899.
Photographer: **Paul Chesley,** United States

Thai classical architecture, most easily seen in the numerous temples within Bangkok, is well known for its splendor of decoration.

Right (top): A wall of gilded guardians from Thai classical mythology protects the Temple of the Emerald Buddha.
Photographer: **Yow Yun Woh,** Singapore

Right (center): Detail of the spectacular multi-tiered roof at the Grand Palace in Bangkok.
Photographer: **Luca Invernizzi Tettoni,** Italy

Right: A saffron-robed monk decorating the gilded *chedi* of Wat Phra That, Doi Suthep in Chiang Mai Province.
Photographer: **Rosine Mazin,** France

The architecture of contemporary Bangkok is nothing if not eclectic, a blend of old and new, classical and what can only be described as whimsy. The angular patterns *(left)* are part of the Zuellig Building, under construction, while the amalgam of neo-classic and sleek modern *(above, left)* is the Wall Street Tower. The Bank of Asia headquarters on South Sathorn Road *(above, right)* is a 19-story structure shaped like a robot, which the architect, Khun Sumet, describes as having "an element of humor" while also being highly practical.
Photographer: **Joe Brignolo,** United States

Above: An ornamental gate opens onto the elegant Suanphlu Gardens.
Photographer: **Leonard Lueras,** United States

Right: Tall buildings, once a rarity in Bangkok's swampy terrain, have now become commonplace, creating an entirely new skyline in the last decade or so. In March 1987, the Baiyoke Tower at Pratunam enjoyed the distinction of being the city's tallest: 150 meters with 43 floors of offices and apartments. Atop the towering structure are the men responsible for the building (from left to right): Sinn Phonghanyudh, the project manager; Sapark Aksharanvgraha, the architect; and Boonrit K. Dilokrat, the project architect.

Next double page: A view of Bangkok by night, showing its ceaseless traffic as well as one of the flyovers built in an effort to ease congestion.

Photographer: **Barrie Rokeach,** United States

Barrie Rokeach

Above (top): Like characters from some futuristic film, hip young motorcyclists pose astride their gaudy machines in the Patpong area, the center of Bangkok's swinging nightlife with its neon-bright spots.
Photographer: **Hiroshi Suga,** Japan

Above: Motorized tricycles, known as *tuks tuks,* offer cheap transportation thrills on Bangkok streets. They replaced the slow-moving pedicabs about 30 years ago.
Photographer: **Gerald Gay,** Singapore

Right: Food stalls along the streets of Bangkok offer a wide variety of delicacies from fragrant meatballs to spicy Thai curries.
Photographer: **Hiroshi Suga,** Japan

Above: The Limelight Bar is one of numerous establishments in the Patpong district offering music and scantily-clad girls, or even bunnies, to draw the customers.
Photographer (top): **Leonard Lueras,** United States
Photographer (bottom): **Hiroshi Suga,** Japan

Right: The crowds along Soi Cowboy show that this is another popular area for enjoying after-dark action in the capital.
Photographer: **Hiroshi Suga,** Japan

Above: Transvestite shows are a popular form of entertainment in Bangkok. Professionally staged and elaborately costumed, they have achieved international renown as well, and some troupes have gone abroad to perform in Germany, France, and Denmark.
Photographer: **Hiroshi Suga,** Japan

Right: Anchalee Chongkhadikij, seen in a recording session, is one of the most popular of the current group of Thai pop singers.
Photographer: **Alberto Cassio,** Italy

Next double page: Discos are big business in Bangkok. Shown here is NASA; it features a real space capsule in addition to laser lighting and top-volume music.
Photographer: **Hiroshi Suga,** Japan

Left: Fashion shows are popular attractions at Bangkok's better hotels. Here Penpak Sirikul, a leading film star and top model, gets some assistance from Ornapa Kritdee.

Above (top): One of Bangkok's leading fashion designers, who signs her creations Pichitra, works on her latest designs in her studio.

Above: Two prominent models — Kara Polasit *(left),* and Spun Selakul.

Photographer: **Alberto Cassio, Italy**

In Thailand, as elsewhere, television has become an essential medium of entertainment as well as of dissemination of information.

Below: The shopkeeper in Nakhon Pathom (top picture) takes time out to view a program, while a member of the Khwanjai family of Bangkok's Chinatown tunes in the set in the family's living-room.
Photographer: **George Mitchell,** United States
Photographer (bottom): **Melinda Berge,** United States

Above: Public sets attract larger audiences, as shown by the crowd collected around this set in the lobby of Siam Center, a popular shopping emporium in downtown Bangkok.
Photographer: **Barrie Rokeach,** United States

Above: Hand-painted signs advertising everything from films to new housing estates add to the color of Bangkok's streets. The top one promotes a show featuring a group of popular local comedians, while another poster depicts the stars of a new Thai movie.
Photographer (top): **Leonard Lueras,** United States
Photographer (bottom): **Richard Kalvar,** United States

Right and next double page: Thai movie theaters are usually adorned with gigantic, hand-painted posters, produced in sections by teams of artists. This painter is working from a publicity still in a studio in Dhonburi.
Photographer (right): **Jean-Leo Dugast,** France
Photographer (next double page): **Alberto Cassio,** Italy

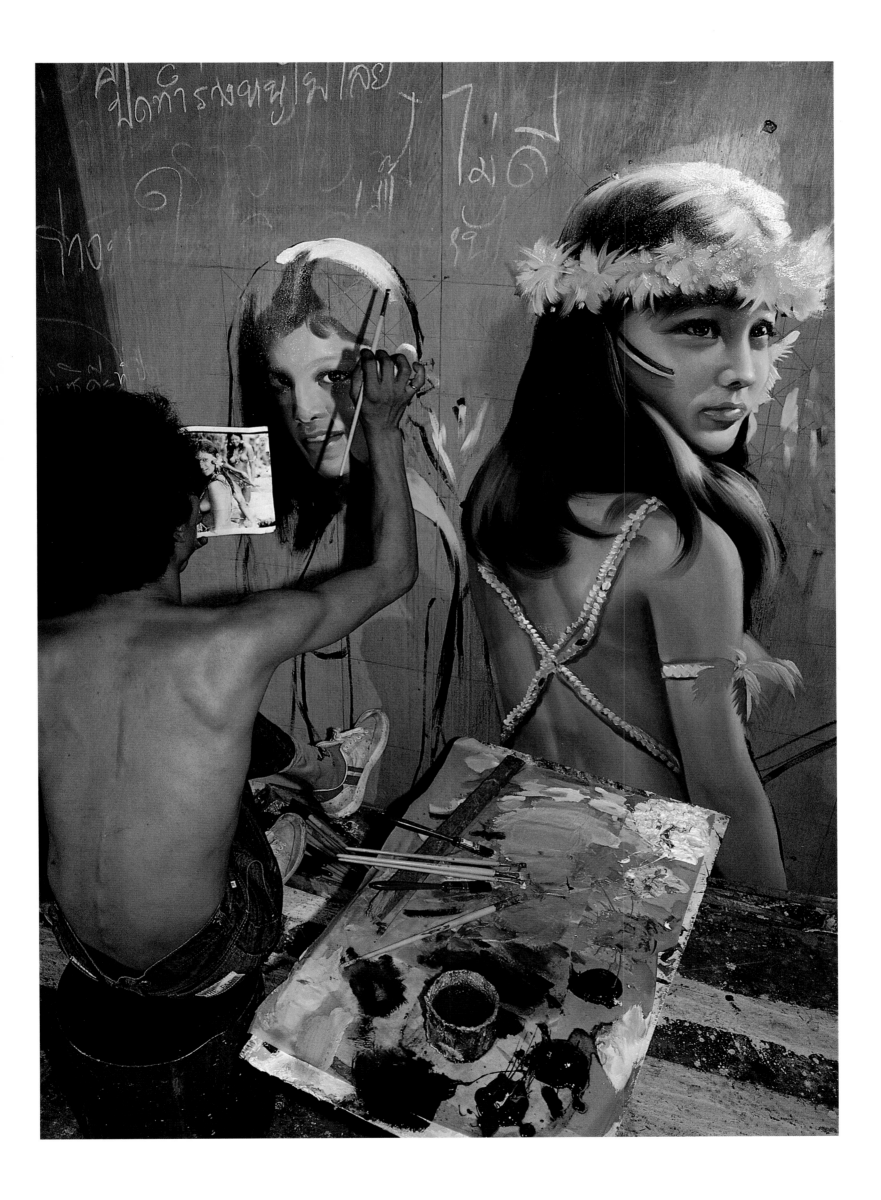

Alberto Cassio

*A*n Ancient Kingdom in Transition

*W*hat most impressed the early photographers who visited Thailand was its rich abundance of exotic beauty, both natural and man-made, and more often than not they turned their lenses on such rewarding subjects as the fabulously ornamented temples, the brooding majesty of a ruined monument, scenic glimpses of busy waterways and tropical luxuriance. Despite all the changes brought by modern development, this is still true. From the densely forested mountains that rise in the far north to the spectacular vistas along the southern coasts, and in artistic achievements extending over a thousand years, the kingdom's aesthetic allure remains one of its greatest attractions, as irresistible to the camera-carrying visitor of today as it was to the traveler of the last century.

Traditionally — and to a large extent even now — the greatest art of Thailand has been Buddhist art, prompted by a fervent desire to earn merit through the carving and casting of Buddha images, the construction of ever more splendid monasteries or religious complexes, and their decoration by masters of glass and porcelain mosaics, mural paintings, gold and black lacquerwork, wood carving, and delicate designs created by mother-of-pearl inlays. The earliest examples, appearing between the first and fifth centuries A.D., were predominantly Indian in style. Later, but before the Thais appeared on the scene, the Mon Dvaravati kingdom produced more original

Left: The Phra Pathom Chedi in Nakhon
Pathom was originally built by the Mons.
Restored in the 19th century it is now elevated
to a height of 127 meters.
Photographer: **Nik Wheeler**, Great Britain

Photographer (above): **Pier Giorgio Sclarandis**, Italy

statuary and monuments, among the most famous examples being the great Phra Pathom Chedi at Nakhon Pathom, now covered by a bell-shaped *chedi* built in the mid-19th century and reputed to be the largest in the world. And still later, the Khmers left an artistic trail of impressive temples, mainly in the northeastern region though also extending deep into the Central Plains.

The first distinctively Thai styles emerged at Sukhothai, established around 1238. This early kingdom, whose Pali name means Dawn of Happiness, occupies a special place in the Thai heart, reverberating still across the centuries. Here it was that paternalistic patterns of kingship were evolved, together with an ideal of freedom and abundance immortalized in a famous stone inscription dating from 1292: "In the water there is fish, in the fields there is rice. The lord of the realm does not levy toll on his subjects. They are free to lead their cattle or ride their horses to engage in trade; whoever wants to trade in elephants, does so; whoever wants to trade in horses, does so; whoever wants to trade in silver or gold, does so." Here, too, was achieved a remarkable fusion of native and outside artistic influences, resulting in temples of grave, almost austere beauty and what most Thais regard as the finest Buddha images their culture has ever produced.

In Ayutthaya, the next capital, power was expressed through splendor, both of size and decoration. Scant traces survive of the urban magnificence that so impressed visitors like the Abbé de Choisy and de la Loubère, the city having been almost entirely destroyed following defeat by the Burmese in 1767; but ample evidence of its cultural brilliance can be seen in ornate images and wonderfully wrought ceremonial objects preserved in Thai museums, and even in ruin its remaining temples and *chedis* are capable of commanding awe.

It can be said that from a technical standpoint, Thai art reached its highest peak toward the end of the Ayutthaya period, when thousands of artisans were involved in decorating the Buddhist kingdom's countless monasteries and palaces. These skills did not perish with the city but survived to enjoy a brief renaissance in the early years of Bangkok, most memorably in the glittering profusion of Wat Phra Keo, a showcase of superb craftsmanship built by Rama I to house the sacred Emerald Buddha and added to by subsequent kings of the Chakri Dynasty. Similar decorative talents were applied to other royal monasteries in the capital such as Wat Phra Chetupon (popularly known as Wat Po), Wat Suthat, and the towering Wat Arun (the Temple of Dawn) overlooking the Chao Phya River.

Beauty was not limited to religious structures, however. The same artisans who

An elderly kite maker continues to produce his elegantly simple creations in Surin Province. *Photographer:* **John Everingham,** Australia

Straw hats, an essential item of clothing for Thai farmers, are a traditional handicraft in the province of Chiang Mai.
Photographer: **Kraipit Phanvut,** Thailand

adorned them also turned out innumerable items for secular use in ordinary as well as aristocratic households: nielloware bowls, betel nut sets in gold and silver, lacquered screens, delicately carved pieces of furniture. Even the traditional domestic Thai house, with its paneled teak walls and steep soaring roof, had an elegance of line as striking in its simplicity as were the *wats* in their ornamentation.

Nor has the tradition of fine handicrafts vanished in an age of mass-produced synthetics. Throughout the kingdom it can be seen still in a wide variety of forms, from the intricately-woven fish traps and baskets used in every village to the magnificent creations of master gold- and silversmiths. When Wat Phra Keo underwent an extensive renovation as part of Bangkok's bicentennial celebration in 1982, there was no great difficulty in rounding up artisans capable of restoring and duplicating the great achievement of their gifted ancestors.

Nature, too, plays an important role in Thailand's visual appeal, contributing a wonderfully assorted collection of scenic effects. Out of the pellucid blue waters of the far south, sheer limestone outcrops rise dramatically like images in a dream, while below lies a silent submarine world of bizarre and brilliant sea creatures. Rainfall is more constant in this part of the kingdom, and in lush jungles secret streams meander toward the sea, great trees strain toward the light through the embrace of tenacious creepers, and the haunting hoots of gibbons echo in the early morning.

Misty mountains dominate the northern landscape, and picturesque villages nestle in secret valleys, watered by rivers whose names sound like the plangent tones of Thai music: Ping, Wang, Yom, Nan. The winter months are cool, and there are thick forests of teak and other hardwood trees, as well as hillsides ablaze with flowers.

Better-known rivers as well figure prominently in the nation's scenery. Along the Laotian border flows the mighty Mekong on part of its 4,335-kilometer journey to the sea off Vietnam. Less impressive in length — only 365 kilometers — yet far more influential in Thai history is the Chao Phya, which moves in lazy loops through the Central Plains, regularly flooding the vital rice fields that have sustained a succession of great kingdoms. Through the fields stretch other, man-made waterways, many of such antiquity that they have acquired a timeless, natural appearance beneath canopies of bushy bamboo and venerable trees.

Enduring in a world of change, Thailand's varied manifestations of beauty constitute a rich heritage to be treasured by future generations. One need not be in the kingdom very long before one comes to appreciate what is being done to keep the traditional Thai arts alive and thriving.

Overleaf: Detail from a mural painting at Wat Nong Bua in Pa Kha, Nan Province, painted between 1867-88.
Photographer: **Rio Helmi,** Indonesia

In the mid-1960s, in the small northeastern village of Ban Chiang in Udon Thani Province, a visitor happened to notice a number of pieces of handsome painted pottery unearthed during road construction. Eventually this resulted in the excavation of sites inhabited 5,000 years ago by a remarkable prehistoric culture whose people cultivated rice, kept domestic animals, wove textiles, and somehow evolved what may have been the world's first knowledge and application of bronze metallurgy.

Left (top): Water jars, at once utilitarian and graceful in shape, are still an essential item in rural households.
Photographer: **John Everingham,** Australia

Left: A group of painted pots found at and around Ban Chiang and now on display at Suan Pakaad, Bangkok.
Photographer: **Luca Invernizzi Tettoni**, Italy

Above: The burial site shown here has been preserved as a memorial to this major archaeological discovery.
Photographer: **Bancha Cheunprapanusorn**, Thailand

Left: Sukhothai saw the development of distinctively Thai styles of architecture and art. Among the surviving examples is this Buddha image in Wat Si Chum.
Photographer: **Michael Freeman,** Great Britain

Above: Homage continues to be paid to this gigantic Reclining Buddha at Wat Lokaya Sutha in Ayutthaya, which became the capital in the 15th century.
Photographer: **Steve Vidler,** Great Britain

Above: The spirit resident of the Erawan Shrine is supposed to have a fondness for
pretty dancing girls, and supplicants whose wishes have been granted often hire several
to give traditional performances in the compound.
Photographer: **Leonard Lueras,** United States

Right: Masks play a prominent part in Thai classical dance, as well as in certain rituals.
Shown here are some bejeweled, brightly-painted masks used in Khon performances.
Photographer: **Diane Garth,** Australia

Left: Likay troupes tour the Thai provinces, often performing at temple fairs. Though classic stories form the basis of their repertoire, these are altered and given local touches to appeal to provincial audiences. This performer is applying make-up for a show at Wat Don in Suphan Buri Province.
Photographer: **Lindsay Hebberd,** United States

Above: These dancers are performing at a celebration held near Wat Mahathat in Nakhon Si Thammarat. The curved fingernails they are wearing originated in the north. The small picture shows one of the dancers waiting for her cue.
Photographer: **Pier Giorgio Sclarandis,** Italy

Above: Mon dancing girls apply make-up during a festival near the Burmese border in Kanchanaburi Province. The Mons arrived in the region around the first century B.C. and exerted a significant influence on the later cultural development of the Thais.
Photographer: **Bill Wassman,** United States

Right: A young boy dancer, in traditional Mon costume, gives a graceful leap during the festivities, held in a village near the Three Pagodas Pass.
Photographer: **Bill Wassman,** United States

Next double page: The village of Bor Sang, not far from Chiang Mai, devotes almost all its energies to the production of hand-painted paper umbrellas.
Photographer: **Rosine Mazin,** France

Page 254: Students from a Phuket school learn to play a traditional bamboo musical instrument, known as the *angkalung,* which came to Thailand from Java, Indonesia.
Photographer: **Nicholas DeVore,** United States

Page 255 (top): A worker applies paint to a Khon mask in the Bangkok studio of the Chit Kaenduangyai family, which has passed the art down through several generations.
Photographer: **Lindsay Hebberd,** United States

Page 255 (bottom): Shadow plays, *nantalung,* are still a popular form of rural entertainment in southern Thailand: the art is believed to have come from Indonesia. The figures are made of leather and have several moveable parts.
Photographer: **Pier Giorgio Sclarandis,** Italy

Page 256: A woman in Nakhon Phanom makes a fish net, probably destined for use in the Mekong River, which flows along the province.
Photographer: **George Mitchell,** United States

Page 257: Using a traditional loom, an old woman in Nakhon Phanom produces a length of silk, one of the most ancient of Thai handicrafts.
Photographer: **George Mitchell,** United States

Pages 258-259: Venerable though these evocative, roofless columns may appear, they are in fact only around twenty years old, part of an imaginative "outdoor museum" called the Ancient City about an hour's drive from Bangkok. Hundreds of such monuments were recreated on the site, which is shaped roughly like Thailand itself.
Photographer: **Wang Miao,** China

Pages 260-261: Near Prasat Muang Sing, a Khmer ruin in Kanchanaburi Province, workers excavate a collection of strange rocks believed by some to be the bones of dinosaurs. Prehistoric remains of early settlers abound in this part of Thailand, many of them found in caves.
Photographer: **Bill Wassman,** United States

Preceding pages: Phu Kradung, or Bell Mountain, rises more than a thousand meters in Loei Province in the northeast. Now a national park, it is a popular destination for hikers, who enjoy its variety of temperate-zone plants and trees — among them pines, azaleas, and rhododendrons — and its scenic waterfalls.
Photographer: **Duangdao Suwanrangsi,** Thailand

Above and right: The Mekong, one of Asia's mightiest rivers, flows along the border dividing Thailand from Laos. The scene above was taken near Mukdahan, the one on the right at Nakhon Phanom. An ambitious plan to tap the river's great resources for the benefit of Thailand and the countries of Indochina has long been on the drawing-board, but remains blocked by war and political divisions.
Photographer: **George Mitchell,** United States

Preceding pages: The boats here are anchored at Koh Phi Phi, a popular tourist attraction that lies in the Andaman Sea about three hours from Phuket. Many visitors to the southern resort island hire such craft to spend a day admiring the scenery and exploring the beauties of the nearby coral reefs. The boats shown in the picture below are also part of Thailand's fishing industry.
Photographer: **Herwarth Voigtmann**, West Germany

A strange and brilliant world of underwater sea creatures is revealed to scuba divers in the coral reefs near Koh Phi Phi in the Andaman Sea. For much of the year, the water here is of exceptional clarity allowing divers to see to great depths.
Photographer: **Herwarth Voigtmann**, West Germany

The beauties of Thailand's far south,
particularly the area along the Andaman Sea,
have made it one of the fastest-growing tourist
attractions in the region. These two pictures
were taken on Koh Phi Phi, a pair of idyllic
islands that lie off the coast, easily accessible by
boat from both Phuket and Krabi. Once
regarded as remote, they are now visited
regularly by tour groups eager to enjoy their
crystalline waters, white-sand beaches, and
dramatic limestone outcrops that rise straight
from the sea. For centuries travelers have come
to collect the edible bird's nests found in a huge
cave on the smaller of the two islands.
Photographer: **Herwarth Voigtmann,**
West Germany

Next double page: In the golden light of sunset,
a boy cycles homeward along a beach in Krabi.
Photographer: **Pier Giorgio Sclarandis,** Italy

APPENDICES

BURMA

Paul Chesley

Steve Vidler

Andaman Sea

Rosine Mazin

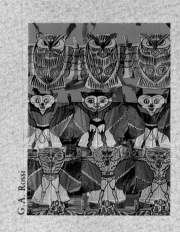

G. A. Rossi

Dominic Sansoni

Joe Carini

INDONESIA

Doi Mae Salong
Leong Ka Tai

Chiang Saen
Rio Helmi

LAOS

Mae Hong Son
Bruno Barbey

Chiang Mai
Rosine Mazin
Kraipit Phanvut
Dominic Sansoni

Lampang
Ping Amranand
John Everingham

Loei
Duangdao Suwanrangsi

Uttaradit
Michael Freeman

Udon Thani
Bancha Cheunprapanusorn

Nakhon Phanom
George Mitchell

Mae Sot
Patrick Gauvain

Melinda Berge
Joe Brignolo
Alberto Cassio
Jean-Leo Dugast
Diane Garth
Lindsay Hebberd
Mike Hosken
Richard Kalvar
Luca Invernizzi Tettoni
Koes
Leonard Lueras
Paul Montri
Raghu Rai
Barrie Rokeach
G.A. Rossi
Hiroshi Suga
Wang Miao
Yow Yun Woh

THAILAND

Lopburi
Steve Vidler

Kanchanaburi
Bill Wassman

Ayutthaya
Paul Chesley

Nakhon Pathom
Nik Wheeler

BANGKOK

Kao Yai National Park
Tom Chuawiwat

Aranyaprathet
Ian Berry

VIETNAM

Hua Hin
Mark Howard

Pattaya
Hyacinthe Cao

KAMPUCHEA

Chanthaburi
Gerald Gay

Gulf of Thailand

Koh Samui
Bernard Hermann

Surat Thani
Pisit Jiropas

Yow Yun Woh

Phang Nga Bay
Andris Apse

Nakhon Si Thammarat
Pier Giorgio Sclarandis

Phuket
Nicholas DeVore III

Koh Phi Phi
Herwarth Voigtmann

Songkhla
Franco Salmoiraghi

Hat Yai
Joe Carini

G.A. Rossi

Narathiwat
Abbas

MALAYSIA

Date/Programme		Venue
1st March, Sunday		
09.00am	**GROUP PHOTOGRAPH** Photographers leave hotel by 08.30am to pose with over 60 tuk tuks at Sanum Luang for a group picture. After the shoot, the train of tuk tuks, escorted by tourist police will return to the Regent.	Sanum Luang
12.00pm	**ASSIGNMENT CEREMONY** Brief ceremony to give all photographers an overall picture of THAILAND: 7 Days in the Kingdom. Photographers will also receive their 60 rolls of film, caption books, vests and other supplies from the sponsors.	Regent Hotel Ratanakosin Rm
05.00pm	**PRESS CONFERENCE** Attended by Thai and foreign media.	Regent Hotel Ratanakosin Rm
06.30pm	**COCKTAIL PARTY HOSTED BY KODAK** The evening's entertainment will be by a traditional Thai drum music group.	Regent Hotel Pimarnman Rm
08.30pm	**WORKING DINNER PARTY** A special performance by a Thai dance group has been arranged. Hosted by Times Editions and the Regent of Bangkok.	Regent Hotel Swimming Pool
2nd March, Monday		
07.00am	**BLESSING FROM THAI MONKS** At 06.00am the thai monks will break their fast and at 07.00am they will begin the ceremony. It will last for half an hour.	Regent Hotel Amorn Room
9th March, Monday		
04.00pm	**AUTOGRAPH PARTY** 14 photographers and 2 writers working for Thailand '87 project have already published books with Times Editions/Les Editions Du Pacifique. They will autograph their books, altogether 22 different titles, at the party.	Asia Book Store Peninsula Plaza
06.00pm	**COCKTAIL PARTY** Informal party hosted by Asia Book Store.	Asia Book Store Peninsula Plaza
08.00pm	**FAREWELL DINNER BUFFET PARTY** Buffet dinner attended by photographers, organizers and invited guests. Hosted by Times Editions and the Regent of Bangkok.	Regent Hotel Swimming Pool

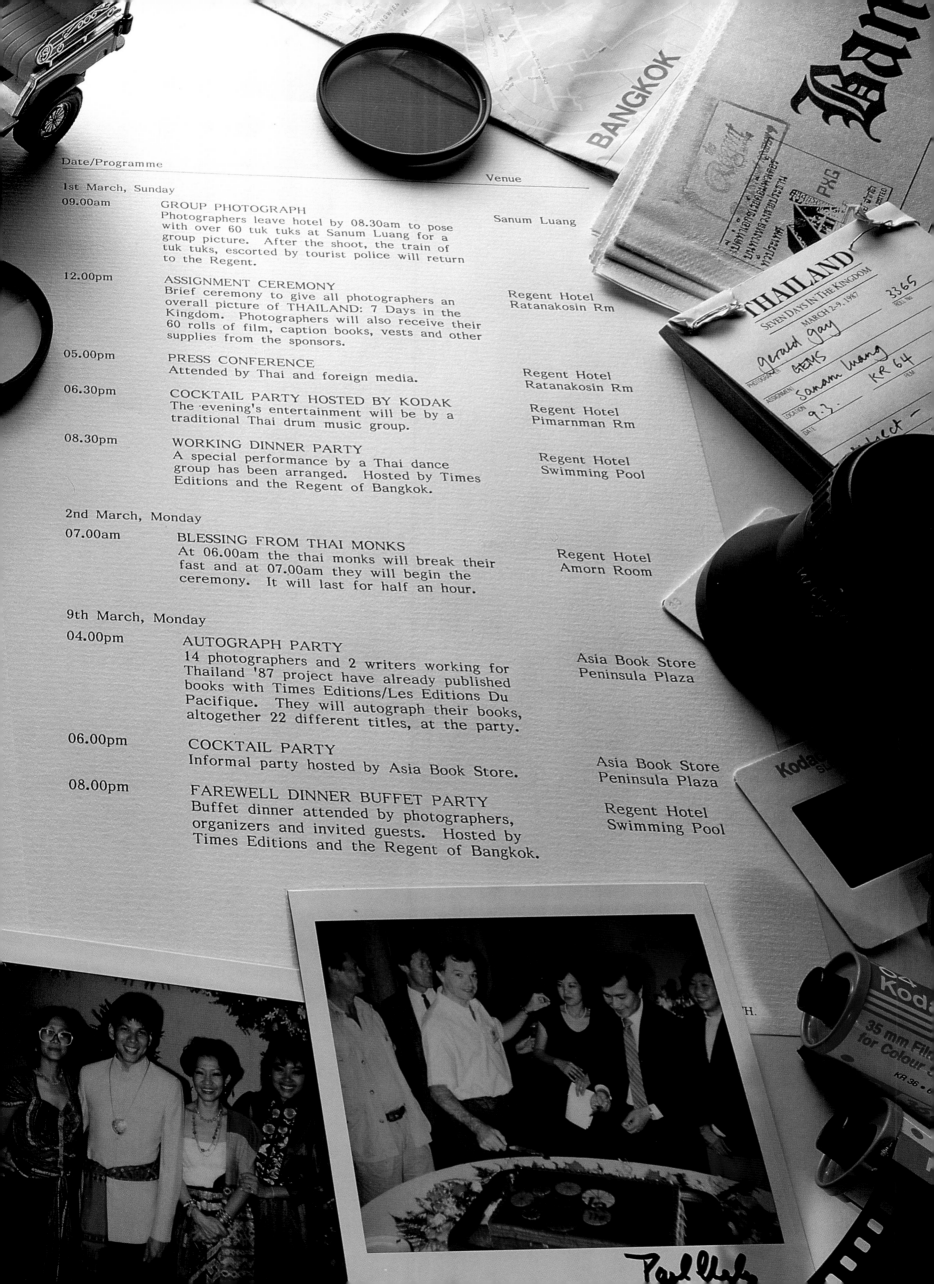

Behind the Shutters

Abbas, Iran
A "Third-Worlder" now living in the West, Abbas has covered major political events in Africa, the Middle East, the Far East, Latin America and Europe since 1970. He spent a year photographing Mexico. A member of the prestigious Magnum Photo Agency, he recently won the first Olivier Rebbot Award.
Assignment: Muslim communities in Bangkok, Pattani and Narathiwat.

Ping Amranand, Thailand
Born in Thailand, Ping now freelances in Washington D.C. specializing in editorial and corporate photography. His work has appeared in *The Washington Post* and numerous leisure, travel and general interest publications such as *House & Garden,* and *Architectural Digest.* He has held one-man shows in Thailand and the United States.
Assignment: A traditional monastery at Lampang Luang.

Andris Apse, New Zealand
Apse is one of New Zealand's most distinguished landscape photographers. He has lectured widely and has served as a judge at the prestigious Australian Arts Council Photographic Competition. Apse has won many awards for his work. His most recent book, *New Zealand from the Air,* is published by Times Editions.
Assignment: Koh Panyi, a Muslim village in Phang Nga Bay.

Andris Apse at Phang Nga Bay.

Bruno Barbey, France
Barbey has been a member of the Magnum Photo Agency since 1966. He has covered stories on every continent and his work is regularly featured in *Life, The Sunday Times* (London), *Stern, National Geographic, GEO* and *Paris Match.* A winner of many prestigious awards, he has exhibited his work in Paris, London, Rome and Zurich.
Assignment: Hilltribes and Shan people in Mae Hong Son Valley.

Melinda Berge with Thai guides.

Melinda Berge, United States
Berge is one of the founding partners of Photographers/Aspen, a highly acclaimed assignment agency and stock photo library based in Aspen, Colorado.
She is a winner of the Lowell Award. Her work appears regularly in *National Geographic, Paris Match, Moda* and *GEO.* Her photographs have also been seen in major shows, the most recent at the Journey into Imagination Pavilion at Disneyworld's Epcot Center.
Assignment: Schools, hospitals, housing and family life in Bangkok.

Bernard Hermann and Joe Brignolo.

Ian Berry, Great Britain
Included in *World Photography: 25 Great Photographers* and a winner of the 1977 Nikon Photographer of the Year Award, Berry has held major exhibitions of his work in London, Paris, Tokyo and Hamburg over a 25-year career. A member of Magnum since 1963, his most recent show "South Africa", held in Paris, won him much respect and recognition.
Assignment: Refugee camps.

Bruno Barbey.

ZCZC
0002
URGENT
SEVENDAYS

EXBKK 3 - 10
RA

THAILAND CAPTIVATES TOP PHOTOGRAPHERS
BY CIMI SUCHONTAN, THE BANGKOK POST

BANGKOK (SPECIAL) - THE INVITATIONS WENT OUT IN FEBRUARY -- JUST A MONTH BEFORE SHOOTING WAS TO BEGIN. NEVERTHELESS, THE ASSIGNMENT -- A WEEK TRYING TO CAPTURE THE SPECIAL BEAUTY AND UNIQUE CHARM OF THAILAND -- WAS ENOUGH TO LURE HARD-TO-GET PHOTOGRAPHERS AWAY FROM THEIR WORK IN EUROPE, AMERICA, ASIA AND THE PACIFIC. THEY ARRIVED IN BANGKOK BEFORE MARCH 1 AS ENTHUSIASTIC AS THEY WERE BLEARY-EYED. IN SEVEN DAYS, 50 PHOTOGRAPHERS, INCLUDING 10 FROM THAILAND, WERE TO COVER 73 PROVINCES, FREEZING ON FILM, FOR ETERNITY, LIFE IN THE THAI KINGDOM AS THEY FOUND IT DURING THE FIRST WEEK OF MARCH 1987.

BUT TRUE TO THEIR PENCHANT FOR SANUK, FUN, THE THAIS, AS IF SPRINGING A SURPRISE, WERE READY FOR THEM. THEY HAD BEEN WARN- BY PRE-SHOOT PUBLICITY THAT THE SEVEN DAYS IN THE KINGDOM LENSMEN WOULD BE A TALENTED BUT ECCENTRIC LOT.

MORE

87 1805G)

Joe Brignolo, United States
For the past 16 years, Brignolo has circled the world on assignments as a top advertising and corporate photographer. He shoots about 38,000 pictures a year. His clients include giants like General Electric, IBM, Texaco, Dupont and Caltex. Represented by Image Bank, Brignolo has held many one-man exhibitions. He recently published *Manhattan,* a personal and detailed observation of the island.
Assignment: Bangkok as a fast-growing city and port, also industry on the eastern seaboard.

Hyacinthe Cao, Tahiti
Cao has worked as a fashion photographer for *Vogue, Mode-International,* and couturiers like Guerlain and Christian Dior. UTA, Peugeot, L'oreal and Climat de France have also used his work. Now a full-time photographer and film-maker, he lives in Papeete, where he is a member of the Tahiti Tourist Promotion Board photography team.
Assignment: Pattaya's beaches and nightlife.

Joe Carini, United States
Originally from Milwaukee, Wisconsin, Carini has found his paradise in Hawaii, where he is busy preserving Hawaiian culture through his lens.
His superb work on hula dancers has appeared in publications like *GEO, Merian* and several books titled *Images of Hawaii* and including *Hawaii: The Big Island.* He is also a corporate photographer for clients such as Hawaiian Airlines, Amfac, Hyatt Hotels and Hotel Corporations of the Pacific.
Assignment: Trains, a vital transportation mode in Thailand.

Alberto Cassio, Italy
Cassio is considered the leading fashion photographer in Bangkok, where he has been based since 1977. His work is seen regularly in *Looks,* a popular Thai magazine, as well as in many regional inflight magazines. Book credits include titles on Australia, Maldives and most recently *Thailand: A View from Above* published by Times Editions. Cassio also works as a corporate and advertising photographer.
Assignment: The Thai entertainment industry; movie stars and fashion.

Paul Chesley, United States
Presently living in Aspen, Colorado, Chesley has been a freelance photographer with the National Geographic Society since 1975 traveling throughout Japan, Europe, South America and the United States. Solo exhibitions of his work have been held in the USA and Japan, including a 1984 show at the Academy of Arts in Honolulu. His pictures can be seen in publications such as *Fortune, GEO, Smithsonian, Esquire* and *Time.*
Assignment: Life on the Chao Phya River between Bangkok and Ayutthaya.

Bancha Cheunprapanusorn, Thailand
Bancha has been a commercial photographer for the past 10 years. He is a member of the Tourism Authority of Thailand's photography team. His pictures can be seen in many Asian publications and travel guides. He is also a freelance writer and a member of the Pacific Area Travel Association.
Assignment: Lifestyles and landscape in the northeast.

Didier Millet, Nicholas DeVore, Lindsay Hebberd, John Everingham and Tom Chuawiwat at Sanam Luang.

Tom Chuawiwat, Thailand
A former painter turned photographer, Chuawiwat is well-known in Asia for his work on his home country, Thailand. He spent many years as an advertising photographer before establishing his own studio in Bangkok. He has held several one-man shows in Bangkok and recently published *A Portrait of Thailand* and *The Life of the Lord Buddha from Thai Mural Paintings.*
Assignment: Kao Yai National Park and the Chokchai Ranch.

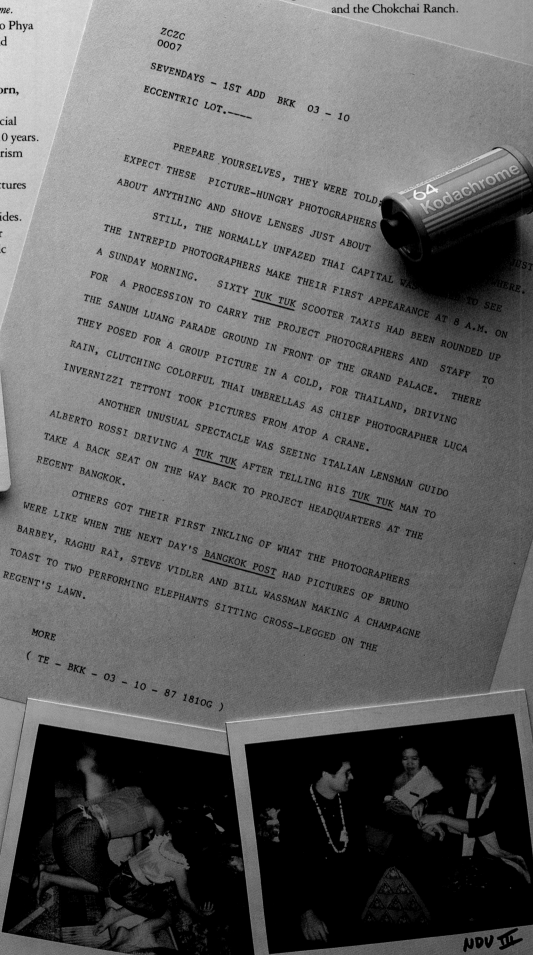

ZCZC
0007

SEVENDAYS - 1ST ADD BKK 03 - 10
ECCENTRIC LOT.____

PREPARE YOURSELVES, THEY WERE TOLD; EXPECT THESE PICTURE-HUNGRY PHOTOGRAPHERS ABOUT ANYTHING AND SHOVE LENSES JUST ABOUT STILL, THE NORMALLY UNFAZED THAI CAPITAL WAS JUST TO SEE THE INTREPID PHOTOGRAPHERS MAKE THEIR FIRST APPEARANCE AT 8 A.M. ON A SUNDAY MORNING. SIXTY TUK TUK SCOOTER TAXIS HAD BEEN ROUNDED UP FOR A PROCESSION TO CARRY THE PROJECT PHOTOGRAPHERS AND STAFF TO THE SANUM LUANG PARADE GROUND IN FRONT OF THE GRAND PALACE. THERE THEY POSED FOR A GROUP PICTURE IN A COLD, FOR THAILAND, DRIVING RAIN, CLUTCHING COLORFUL THAI UMBRELLAS AS CHIEF PHOTOGRAPHER LUCA INVERNIZZI TETTONI TOOK PICTURES FROM ATOP A CRANE.
ANOTHER UNUSUAL SPECTACLE WAS SEEING ITALIAN LENSMAN GUIDO ALBERTO ROSSI DRIVING A TUK TUK AFTER TELLING HIS TUK TUK MAN TO TAKE A BACK SEAT ON THE WAY BACK TO PROJECT HEADQUARTERS AT THE REGENT BANGKOK.
OTHERS GOT THEIR FIRST INKLING OF WHAT THE PHOTOGRAPHERS WERE LIKE WHEN THE NEXT DAY'S BANGKOK POST HAD PICTURES OF BRUNO BARBEY, RAGHU RAI, STEVE VIDLER AND BILL WASSMAN MAKING A CHAMPAGNE TOAST TO TWO PERFORMING ELEPHANTS SITTING CROSS-LEGGED ON THE REGENT'S LAWN.

MORE

(TE - BKK - 03 - 10 - 87 1810G)

Lindsay Hebberd and Nicholas DeVore.

Michael Freeman and Jean-Leo
Dugast keeping dry.

Nicholas DeVore III,
United States
Born in Paris, presently living in
Aspen, Colorado and working all
over the world, DeVore has for the
past 15 years traveled widely to take
pictures for publications like
National Geographic, lecture on
photography, or expand his stock
files. A member of the Explorer's
Club, and the Board of Trustees
for the Aspen Art Museum, DeVore
is also a principal partner of
Photographers/Aspen.
Assignment: Phuket, the resort,
the tin mines and the rubber
plantations.

Jean-Leo Dugast, France
Dugast has been living in Asia for
the past 12 years and has been
working as a full-time photographer
for the last four years. His work,
distributed by Sygma in Paris, has
appeared in publications like *Grand
Reportages, GEO, Corto, Newlook* and
Sud-est-Asia. He has held two
exhibitions in France and recently
completed a two-year journey
through India, Sri Lanka and
Southeast Asia.
Assignment: Thai Mysticism,
ceremonies and rituals.

John Everingham, Australia
A freelance photographer now living
in Thailand, Everingham's coverage
of the Vietnam War appeared in
*Newsweek, Far Eastern Economic
Review* and *The Australian.*
More recently he has been
contributing regularly to
publications such as *National
Geographic, Smithsonian* and *GEO.*
Assignment: Elephants, elephant
schools and the traditional
employment of elephants.

Michael Freeman, Great Britain
A professional since 1973, Freeman
has built a reputation as a special
effects photographer contributing
regularly to publications such as
*GEO, Smithsonian, Sunday Times
Magazine, Time* and *Life.*
He is the author of many titles
including *The 35mm Handbook* and
The Studio Manual. He has held
many exhibitions, the latest being a
"Creative Futures" show held in
London.
Assignment: Life in Lap Lae, a
Thai village, and Sukhothai.

Photographers take to *tuk tuks.*

Diane Garth, Australia
A corporate photographer and an
aerial specialist, Garth has worked
on assignments for Australian
organizations such as the Sydney
Morning Herald, New South Wales
Department of Housing and the
Westpac Banking Corporation. Her
work can also be seen in Times
Editions' *Indonesia from the Air.*
She has held several photographic
exhibitions, some in conjunction
with the Institute of Architects in
New South Wales.
Assignment: Thai International
operations.

Paul Chesley
THAILAND: 7 DAYS IN THE KINGDOM

April 7th, 1987 - Chiloe Island - Chile
Aloha Howdy Leonardo Love:
No massages, few hot baths - sushi none.
Autumn wind brings winter short thru
Patagonia. Hawks overhead - giant trout
below - Easter Island too far to swim.
Enjoyed so much playing with you
Leonard. That was a grand project -
a pleasure and delight to share. thank
you beaucoups for your camraderie and
cheer.
Thinking of you - busy edit, late
nights - warm weather.
Keen to rendezvous another sooncome -
plan ahead New Mexico boy.
Amitiés and Mahalo,
Nicholas

SAN CARLOS DE BARILOCHE - Rep. Argentina
El Casco
Gran terraza
Foto Juan Hinbar

Señor Leonardo La
Times Editions
422 Thomson Rd
Singapore 1129

Patrick Gauvain, Great Britain
Based in Thailand since 1968,
Gauvain worked as a creative
director and freelance photographer
till he founded Shrimp Studios in 1977.
An advertising and corporate
photographer, Gauvain's work has
appeared in films for the Tourism
Authority of Thailand and in a
multi-media presentation for the
1979 PATA conference in Seoul. He
was an assistant director for movies
like The Man with the Golden Gun
and Deerhunter.
Assignment: Setting up a traveling
studio in the north.

Patrick "Shrimp" Gauvain.

SEVENDAYS - 2ND ADD BKK 03 - 10
REGENT'S LAWN.----

A THAI-LANGUAGE DAILY WENT SO FAR AS TO WARN THE
PUBLIC THAT SOME OF THE PHOTOGRAPHERS WERE THAIS. "IF YOU
SEE A SILVER-HAIRED PHOTOGRAPHER LURKING AROUND," IT WARNED
ON ITS FRONT PAGE, "DON'T SWEAR AT HIM IN THAI BECAUSE HIS NAME
IS PAUL MONTRI AND HE WILL UNDERSTAND EVERY NASTY WORD YOU SAY."
MONTRI, OF THAI-GERMAN PARENTAGE, RAISED AN EYEBROW AND
BLUSHED WHEN HE SAW HIS PICTURE IN THE PAPER.
BEING RECOGNIZED WAS NO DISADVANTAGE FOR JAPAN'S HIROSHI
SUGA, WHO FOUND HIMSELF QUITE POPULAR ALONG HIS BEAT -- THE CITY'S
PATPONG ROAD NIGHT SPOTS. "EVEN THE BARGIRLS HAD READ ABOUT US IN
THE PAPERS," HE CHUCKLED.
AFTER THEIR FIRST DAY IN THAILAND, A FEW OF THE VETERAN
PHOTOJOURNALISTS ALREADY APPEARED SHELL-SHOCKED, AND THEY HADN'T
EVEN BEGUN THEIR ASSIGNMENTS. BUT, LUCKY FOR THEM, A COMMAND
CENTER HAD BEEN SET UP ON THE FOURTH FLOOR OF THE REGENT, WHERE
AMID CONSTANT NEAR-CHAOS, PROJECT COORDINATORS HAD PLACED A GIANT
MAP OF THAILAND WITH BLACK DOTS THAT REPRESENTED THE PLACES WHERE
THE LENS-ARMED TROOPERS WERE SUPPOSED TO GO -- NAMELY ALL OVER
THE PLACE.

MORE

(TF - BKK - 03

Organizers and photographers gather at Sanam Luang, in front of the Grand Palace, for a drizzly, group portrait.

Gerald Gay, Singapore
Gay specializes in still-life and advertising photography. A partner of Developing Agents Photography. Singapore, since 1986, his pictures can be seen in Times Editions' *Best of Mauritian Cooking, Cuisine Reunionnaire* and *The New Art of Indonesian Cooking*.
Assignment: Jewelry and mining in Thailand.

Lindsay Hebberd, United States
Hebberd is a freelance photographer who specializes in documenting cultures and traditions. A regular contributor to *National Geographic,* she has traveled extensively in Asia, Africa and the Americas. She recently held an exhibition entitled "Portraits of Southwest American Indians" in the USA and is currently working on a new theme, "Faces of Asia". She was a bronze medal winner in the NPCI contest in 1985.
Assignment: Likay folk theatre.

Rio Helmi, Indonesia
Helmi began freelance photography in 1978, working mainly in black-and-white, photographing people within the context of their traditional cultures and environment. A photographer/editor with the Indonesian fortnightly news magazine *Mutiara* till 1985, he is presently working on two book projects on West Sumba and Bali, Indonesia.
Assignment: Chiang Saen and Chiang Rai districts.

Bernard Hermann, France
Hermann began his photographic career working for major European newspapers and then established himself as a full-time professional, traveling and working to produce titles on Guadeloupe, Haiti and Tahiti.
He has also worked with Times Editions on the city series of pictorial albums about San Francisco, Rio de Janeiro, New York, Paris, New Orleans and Sydney.
Assignment: Koh Samui.

Bernard Hermann.

Mike Hosken, New Zealand
Originally from Auckland, Hosken now lives in New Caledonia. He has been involved with photography and design work for almost 19 years. His pictures, which reflect his favorite pastimes of sailing and fishing, and his interest in the outdoors and animals, have appeared in *Hi-Wind* and *GEO*.
He is also the co-author of the first book on New Caledonia — *Nouvelle-Calédonie: Ile de Lumières* — and is presently working on another book, *New Caledonia from the Air,* for Times Editions.
Assignment: Trucks and trucking.

Rio Helmi and Leonard Lueras.

Mark Howard, Great Britain
Howard was born and raised in Thailand before going to England for his studies. He worked in London and traveled to the USA and the Middle East, before returning to Thailand to work as a professional photographer.
His pictures have appeared in advertisements and several travel magazines in the region such as Thai International's *Sawasdee* magazine.
Assignment: Phetchaburi province and Hua Hin.

Mark Howard.

281

Luca Invernizzi Tettoni, Italy
Born in Northern Italy, Tettoni has worked extensively throughout Asia as an advertising and travel photographer. He won the 1985 PATA Professionalism Award for "Specific Contribution to the Promotion of Thailand and South East Asia". His work appears in many books, including: *Legendary Thailand, The Arts of Thailand,* and the *Bangkok, Chiang Mai* and *Burma* titles of the Times Travel Library published by Times Editions.
Assignment: Bangkok's Royal Palace.

Pisit Jiropas, Thailand
Pisit began taking photographs 12 years ago and has for the past four years turned his hobby into a full-time occupation. A painter of landscapes and portraits, this decorative arts graduate from Silipakorn University reveals the painter in him.
Assignment: The life of fishermen in Surat Thani.

Luca Invernizzi Tettoni.

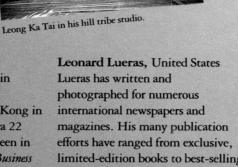
Leong Ka Tai in his hill tribe studio.

Leong Ka Tai, Hong Kong
After embarking on a career in photography in Paris, Leong returned to his native Hong Kong in 1976 and founded his Camera 22 Studio. His pictures can be seen in many magazines including *Business Week,* the *Sunday Observer* and in books such as *China: The Long March, Salute to Singapore* and *Beijing* published by Times Editions.
Assignment: Border police and the Chinese village of Doi Mae Salong.

Leonard Lueras, United States
Lueras has written and photographed for numerous international newspapers and magazines. His many publication efforts have ranged from exclusive, limited-edition books to best-selling titles such as *Surfing: The Ultimate Pleasure,* and more recently *Bali: The Ultimate Island.*
He has spent most of the past 25 years living and working in the Asia Pacific area. He is now the creative director of Times Editions.
Assignment: Street scenes in Bangkok.

Rosine Mazin, France
Paris-born Mazin's breakthrough as a freelancer was a book on Normandy in 1977. Since then, she has been actively working as a photographer and a regular contributor to *Figaro* magazine. In 1984, she published a book containing her most beautiful pictures of Paris. Her current interest is aerial photography and her recent book titles include *Reunion from the Air* and *Mauritius from the Air.*
Assignment: Chiang Mai province.

George Mitchell, United States
An American based in Asia, Mitchell has spent the last 10 years working as a freelance photographer concentrating on corporate and industrial photography. He is most interested in Korea and has followed closely its rapid economic development over the past decade. He recently completed *Seoul* for the Times Travel Library published by Times Editions.
Assignment: Life along the banks of the Mekong River.

Pisit Jiropas.

Richard Kalvar, United States
A graduate of Cornell University in literary studies, Kalvar began working as a photographer in 1970. A full member of Magnum since 1977 and presently vice president for Europe, Kalvar divides his time between Paris, New York and brief spells in Rome, where he is working on a personal project.
Assignment: The military.

Koes, Indonesia
Born, raised and presently working on the island of Bali, Koes began freelance photography more than 14 years ago. His strong interest in travel and advertising photography has taken him to all over Asia, Europe and Australia.
Koes is the 1977 winner of two gold medal awards from the Indonesian Photographic Society.
Assignment: Education, banking and the stock exchange in Bangkok.

Paul Chesley

SEVENDAYS – 3RD ADD BKK 03 – 10

THE LOGISTICS INVOLVED RESEMBLED THOSE NEEDED TO MAKE A MAJOR FEATURE FILM. EACH PHOTO-GRAPHER WAS GIVEN A DETAILED WEEK-LONG SHOOTING ASSIGNMENT, A LARGE QUANTITY OF KODAK FILM, AND OFF THEY WENT, FANNING OUT INTO THE NEAR AND FAR CORNERS OF THE KINGDOM ON VARIOUS MODES OF TRANSPORTATION. FOR A WEEK FROM DAYLIGHT TO DUSK, THE PHONES AT THE COMMAND CENTER RANG LIKE MAD. IT SEEMED AS IF EACH OF THE ASSIGNMENTS HAD TURNED INTO AN ADVENTURE AND THE ADVENTURERS WERE RAVING ON AS IF THEY WERE THE FIRST OF THEIR KIND EVER TO SET EYES ON THE KINGDOM. AN EXCITED PIER GIORGIO SCLARANDIS CALLED FROM THE SOUTHERN TOWN OF NAKHON SI THAMMARAT TO SAY, "SEND MORE FILM!" UP IN THE NORTHERN CAPITAL OF CHIANG MAI, THAI PHOTOGRAPHER KRAIPIT PHANVUT WAS BUSY TAKING PICTURES OF THE ROYAL FAMILY. HE COMMENTED THAT THE NORTHERNERS "HAD NO IDEA WHAT WE WERE DOING, BUT WERE EXCEEDINGLY HELPFUL." MEANWHILE AT A TENSE FRONTLINE BORDER, INDONESIA'S RIO HELMI LEARNED THAT THAIS REJECT AN UNGRANTABLE REQUEST IN A VERY NICE WAY. "AN ARMY RANGER ON THE BORDER WHO FED ME LUNCH WAS VERY HOSPITABLE, BUT HE POLITELY FORBADE ME FROM TAKING PICTURES OF HIM AT THE OUTPOST."

MORE

(TE – BKK – 03

Paul Montri, Thailand
Montri started out as a photographer's assistant in England more than 25 years ago. After extensive travels and sojourns in Europe doing work as a fashion photographer he became one of Thailand's leading advertising photographers, with clients such as Oglivy and Mather, McCann-Erickson and Thai International.
Assignment: Markets and street vendors in Bangkok.

Kraipit Phanvut, Thailand
Kraipit has been the accredited UPI representative in Bangkok covering Thailand and Southeast Asia since 1975. He has been published in *Paris Match, Newsweek* and *Time* and has worked on assignments for *Asiaweek,* SIPA Press in Paris and Photoreporters (New York). He is presently the chief photographer for the AFP International News Photos Agency.
Assignment: The royal family at the Phuphing Palace.

Raghu Rai, India
Rai began work as a photographer in 1964 and since then has been a regular contributor to *Time, Life, GEO, National Geographic* and *Paris Match.* He was invited to join the Magnum Photo Agency in 1976. He has been the picture editor of *India Today* since 1980. Twenty-five of his photographs are in the permanent collection of the Bibliotheque Nationale in Paris. He has published several photography books including *Mother Teresa, Delhi: A Portrait, The Sikhs* and *Indira Gandhi.*
His most recent book, *Taj Mahal,* was published by Times Editions.
Assignment: Bangkok.

Raghu Rai at the Erawan shrine.

Barrie Rokeach, United States
An aerial specialist and a keen flyer, Rokeach has been involved in photography for the last 14 years. He has an MA in Design and Photography from the University of California at Berkeley. A creative artist, his work can be seen in *Ireland: A Week in the Life of a Nation n* and *24 Hours in the Life of Los Angeles.*
Assignment: Aerial photography.

Guido Alberto Rossi, Italy
The Milan-born Rossi started his career as a sports photographer and went on to cover the Middle East (1967) and Vietnam War (1969). He now concentrates on sports and travel. His pictures appear regularly in various Italian magazines such as *Gente Viaggi, Il Piacere, Expression* and *Autocapital.* Since 1978 he has been director of the Image Bank offices in Italy. Recently he has published a retrospective book entitled *Twenty Years in Color.*
Assignment: Sports in Thailand.

Barrie Rokeach with Thai workers.

Franco Salmoiraghi, United States
Salmoiraghi has worked in Hawaii since 1968. He is a frequent contributor to books and magazines published in Hawaii and Asia and exhibits his work regularly in fine arts galleries throughout Hawaii. He has taught photography in several workshops and at the University of Hawaii.
He is currently working on two book projects, *Christmas Island in the South Pacific* and *Waipio Valley* (on the Big Island of Hawaii).
Assignment: A modern monastery, Suan Moke, and an oil rig.

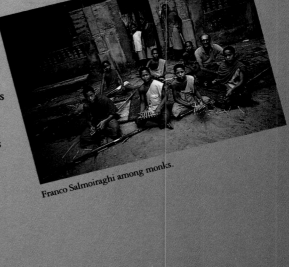
Franco Salmoiraghi among monks.

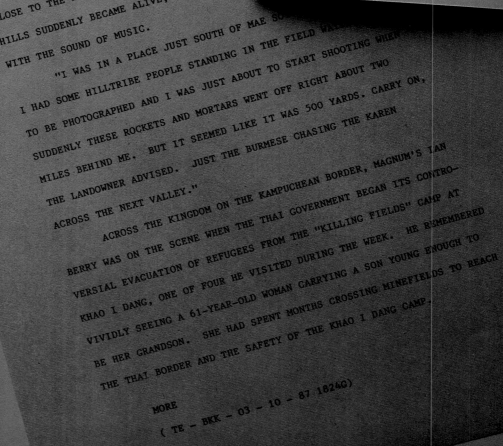

ZCZC
0020
SEVENDAYS - 4TH ADD BKK 03 - 10

THE OUTPOST.——

BANGKOK-BASED STUDIO PHOTOGRAPHER PATRICK GAUVAIN, KNOWN BY THE NAME SHRIMP AND FOR HIS SPICY PIN-UP CALENDARS, WAS CLOSE TO THE BURMESE BORDER WHEN THE HILLS SUDDENLY BECAME ALIVE, BUT NOT WITH THE SOUND OF MUSIC.

"I WAS IN A PLACE JUST SOUTH OF MAE SO I HAD SOME HILLTRIBE PEOPLE STANDING IN THE FIELD WA TO BE PHOTOGRAPHED AND I WAS JUST ABOUT TO START SHOOTING WHEN SUDDENLY THESE ROCKETS AND MORTARS WENT OFF RIGHT ABOUT TWO MILES BEHIND ME. BUT IT SEEMED LIKE IT WAS 500 YARDS. CARRY ON, THE LANDOWNER ADVISED. JUST THE BURMESE CHASING THE KAREN ACROSS THE NEXT VALLEY."

ACROSS THE KINGDOM ON THE KAMPUCHEAN BORDER, MAGNUM'S IAN BERRY WAS ON THE SCENE WHEN THE THAI GOVERNMENT BEGAN ITS CONTRO-VERSIAL EVACUATION OF REFUGEES FROM THE "KILLING FIELDS" CAMP AT KHAO I DANG, ONE OF FOUR HE VISITED DURING THE WEEK. HE REMEMBERED VIVIDLY SEEING A 61-YEAR-OLD WOMAN CARRYING A SON YOUNG ENOUGH TO BE HER GRANDSON. SHE HAD SPENT MONTHS CROSSING MINEFIELDS TO REACH THE THAI BORDER AND THE SAFETY OF THE KHAO I DANG CAMP.

MORE

(TE - BKK - 03 - 10 - 87 1824Q)

Dominic Sansoni, Sri Lanka
Sansoni was selected by the Arts Council of Great Britain to participate in "The New British Image", an exhibition by young photographers in 1978. Now based in Sri Lanka, his pictures can be seen in several inflight magazines such as *Serendib* (Air Lanka) and *Sawasdee* (Thai Airways International). He is presently working on a project in Kathmandu.
Assignment: Chiang Mai province.

Pier Giorgio Sclarandis, Italy
A photographer since 1963, Sclarandis, who founded StillLife advertising in 1968, is associated with Black Star (New York). His pictures are regularly featured in *Gente Viaggi, GEO* and *Grand Reportages.* He has published many photographic books on places such as the Philippines, Hong Kong, Venezuela, the United Arab Emirates and the Dominican Republic.
Assignment: The southern provinces of Nakhon Si Thammarat, Krabi, Phatthalung and Trang.

Hiroshi Suga, Japan
Winner of the 1987 Ken Domon Award, Suga has taken photographs that have appeared in many international publications. His works *Bali Entranced, Bali: The Island of Festivals and Performers,* and *Bali: The Demonic, the Godly and the Wondrous* have received international acclaim. He has held one-man shows in Japan and the United States.
Assignment: Nightlife in Bangkok.

Duangdao Suwanrangsi, Thailand
Duangdao was a permanent writer for the Tourism Authority Magazine in Thailand until she discovered her interest in landscape photography. Since then, she has published several books entitled *The Royal Barge Procession, Phu Luang* and *Back to the Mountains,* a collection of landscape photographs showing four great mountain peaks in northern Thailand.
Assignment: Mountain photography.

Steve Vidler, Great Britain
A native of Dover, Vidler has been a travel photographer for the past 22 years and his principal concern is to produce stock photography for the travel industry. His pictures are widely published in magazines and brochures promoting various destinations. Book credits include works on Switzerland, Peru, and Singapore.
Assignment: Ayutthaya and Lopburi.

Herwarth Voigtmann, West Germany
An underwater specialist, Voigtmann started his own scuba diving school on the Salerne Gulf in 1971.
His spectacular work with sea animals, especially sharks, has won him international recognition as a pioneer and master in underwater photography. He lives in the Maldives on the island of Bandos.
Assignment: The island of Koh Phi Phi.

Pier Giorgio Sclarandis.

Hiroshi Suga.

```
ZCZC
0025

SEVENDAYS - 5TH ADD BKK  03 - 10

KHAO I DANG____


      ASPEN-BASED MELINDA BERGE, WHO HAD BEEN SHOOTING THE
LONELINESS OF THE PITCAIRN ISLANDS A FEW WEEKS EARLIER, WAS
SURPRISED WHEN SHE POPPED IN ON A THAI WEDDING AND SAW MORE THAN A
FEW FRIENDLY FACES.  "IN BANGKOK, THEY DO THINGS IN A BIG WAY," SHE
SAID.  "THERE MUST HAVE BEEN 5,000 PEOPLE THERE!!"
      FRANCE'S JEAN-LEO DUGAST SNAPPED AWAY AT WHAT UNFOLDED WHEN
HE ENTERED THE UNCANNY WORLD OF THE OCCULT.  "AT THE END OF A
KHRAWB KHRU RITE FOR A TATTOOIST, MOST OF THE 30 MEN IN THE ROOM
WENT INTO A DEEP TRANCE AT THE SAME MOMENT.  THEY JUMPED, SHOUTED
AND BEHAVED LIKE TIGERS, PIGS OR MONKEYS," HE RELATED AS IF HE HAD
JUST WOKEN UP FROM A BAD DREAM.
      IMAGINE MIKE HOSKEN'S SURPRISE WHEN THE DELICACY BEING
ENJOYED BY SOME THAI TRUCKERS AT AN EARLY MORNING ROADSIDE BARBECUE
TURNED OUT TO BE GRILLED RODENT!  "THE DRIVERS HANDED ME A SKEWER,"
SAID THE NEW ZEALANDER, "BUT I SAID IT WAS TOO EARLY FOR ME."
      CHINA'S WANG MIAO FELT MORE AT HOME WITH THE SIGHTS AND
SOUNDS OF BANGKOK'S CHINATOWN, ALTHOUGH SHE EXPERIENCED A SENSE OF
DEJA VU AS IT WAS MORE TRADITIONAL IN MANY WAYS THAN CHINA ITSELF.
"I NEVER EXPECTED THE CHINESE IN CHINATOWN HERE WOULD PRESERVE AND
OBSERVE SO MUCH TRADITION.  MOST OF THAT IS GONE ON THE MAINLAND."

  MORE

( TE - BKK - 03 - 10 - 87 1829G)
```

```
FROM: DOMINIC SANSONI
THANKYOU FOR YOUR WONDERFUL AND KIND OFFER - YES - I WOUL
LOVE TO PARTICIPATE IN THAILAND 87 AND WILL WRITE
WITH ALL FURTHER INFORMATION IMMEDIATELY.
      ALSO HOPE NEPAL WILL BE A REALITY IN APRIL.
            BEST REGARDS AND AYUBOWAN

      DOMINIC SANSONI.++
```

Wang Miao.

Wassman.

Nik Wheeler.

Wang Miao, China
A Peking-born correspondent now based in Hong Kong with the China-Hong Kong Tourism Press, Wang has been a photographer for over 10 years. She recently completed a project on Tibet and a book project with the China Modern Photo Salon 1986 titled *Flashback: A Decade of Changes.*
Assignment: Bangkok's Chinatown.

Bill Wassman, United States
An anthropology graduate from the University of San Francisco, Wassman has been involved in editorial and advertising photography since 1970. He has journeyed extensively throughout Nepal, Southeast Asia, Central America and Europe and only recently followed nomads into the Chang Tang region of Tibet. He has taken on assignments for *Signature, Adventure Travel,* Apa *Insight Guides* and others.
Assignment: Kanchanaburi and the Three Pagodas Pass region.

Nik Wheeler, Great Britain
A former UPI representative now represented by Black Star (New York) and SIPA Press (Paris), Wheeler has been based in Los Angeles since 1977. His pictures appear often in *Time, GEO, National Geographic* and *Life.*
Book titles include *Return to the Marshes, Land of Two Rivers, This is China* and *The Bhotias of Nepal.*
Assignment: The floating market in Nakhon Pathom.

Yow Yun Woh, Singapore
A keen photographer since his boyhood, Yow joined the Straits Times Press, Singapore, in 1968 and is presently its chief photographer. His pictures can be seen in the Times group of newspapers as well as in the Times Organisations publication, *Salute to Singapore.* Among other assignments Yow has also covered two visits to China by Singapore Prime Minister Lee Kuan Yew.
Assignment: Temples in Bangkok.

```
ZCZC
0029

SEVENDAYS - 6TH ADD BKK 03 - 10

THE MAINLAND.----

              IN A BLEARY-EYED WAY REMINISCENT OF THE MANNER
        IN WHICH THEY HAD ARRIVED, THE PHOTOGRAPHERS
     CONVERGED ON BANGKOK ON MARCH 9.  THEY GAVE THEIR
   ROLLS OF FILM -- CONTAINING MORE THAN 85,000 SHOTS
  OF ONE OF THE WORLD'S MOST PHOTOGENIC COUNTRIES -- TO
 CREATIVE DIRECTOR LEONARD LUERAS, WHO SAID IT WOULD BE
 HIS TASK TO TURN THEM INTO "A TIME CAPSULE" -- THIS BOOK.
    UNABLE TO ATTEND THE FAREWELL PARTY WAS BARRIE ROKEACH, THE
  AMERICAN AERIAL PHOTOGRAPHY SPECIALIST WHO HAD HUNG AROUND
 FORLORNLY FOR MOST OF THE WEEK WAITING FOR AN AIRCRAFT AND A PERMIT
 TO SHOOT.  HE WAS READY TO PACK UP AND LEAVE WHEN THE CALL CAME
 THROUGH -- A HELICOPTER AND PILOT WERE WAITING FOR HIM.  "THIS
  PLACE," HE SAID WITH A GRIN, "IS FULL OF SURPRISES."
      HE WAS AIRBORNE WHEN THE OTHERS WERE PREPARING TO LEAVE THE
  KINGDOM AFTER AN EVENTFUL SEVEN DAYS, HAVING SEEN AND EXPERIENCED
 HOW WE SEE THINGS AND HOW WE LIVE.  LIKE OTHER THAIS I'D LIKE TO
 THINK THAT THE PHOTOGRAPHERS LEFT THE KINGDOM HAVING LEARNED SOME-
  THING ABOUT OUR 700-YEAR-OLD TRADITIONS, AND OUR GENTLE, GRACEFUL
   WAY OF LIFE, WHERE PEACE AND HARMONY TRANSCEND ALL.



             END
       ( TE - BKK - 03 - 10 - 87 1838G )
```

AUTHOR

William Warren, a native of the state of Georgia, worked in publishing and television in New York before making Bangkok his home in 1960. Since then, he has divided his time between lecturing in English at the prestigious Chulalongkorn University and writing about Thai culture. Two of his books, *The House on the Klong* and *The Legendary American,* are about silk merchant Jim Thompson, who disappeared in 1967. Among his other books are *Bangkok, Images of Thailand,* and *Thailand from the Air.* His writing has also appeared in the *Reader's Digest, Esquire, Pacific, Asia* and the *New York Times Magazine.*

FOREWORD WRITER

Gore Vidal, born in New Hampshire in 1925, has won critical praise over the past 40 years for his novels, plays and essays. His latest novel, *Empire,* follows his popular historical trilogy — *Burr, 1876* and *Lincoln.*

IN MEMORIAM

Paul Montri
November 27, 1938 — May 17, 1987

Still-life pictures in this section (*pages 276-285*) photographed by **Gerald Gay.**

The Sponsors

 TOURISM AUTHORITY OF THAILAND (TAT) plays an important and active role in promoting the Kingdom as a major tourist destination in the world and spares no effort to draw tourists to visit Thailand. The TAT rallied behind this project offering all the help they could give. It is hoped *Thailand: Seven Days in the Kingdom* will go one more step in helping the TAT realise its ultimate goal.

THAI AIRWAYS INTERNATIONAL, born of a partnership between Thai Airways Company and Scandinavian Airlines System in 1959, has blossomed into a respected international airline serving more than 30 countries throughout the world. Wholly Thai-owned since 1977, THAI has pioneered new routes and expects to welcome aboard well over 3 million passengers this year.

 KODAK (THAILAND) LIMITED, established in 1968 as the sole film distributor of Eastman Kodak Company USA, has been a Thai market leader for years. Kodachrome and Ektachrome film were used exclusively by *Thailand: Seven Days in the Kingdom* photographers and the film and slides were developed in Kodak's modern laboratories in Thailand and Hawaii.

◇ Bangkok Bank Limited estab-
The Asian International Bank lished in 1944, is the largest commercial bank in Thailand and Southeast Asia with its network of 333 branches all over the country and 15 overseas branches in major cities of the Far East and world financial centers. In addition to its own foreign representation, the Bangkok Bank Ltd. has some 1,550 correspondent banks throughout the world.

 THE SIAM CEMENT CO., LTD., the parent company of the Siam Cement Group, was established in 1913. The core businesses are cement and refractories, construction materials, machinery, pulp and paper, trading and other businesses.

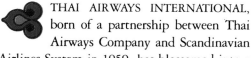 THE REGENT of BANGKOK is the choice of discriminating travelers, who have discovered it to be an oasis of graceful elegance and hospitality in the heart of the bustling City of Angels. A Regent International Hotel, the Regent of Bangkok is meeting the needs of today's modern travelers.

 American Express (Thai) Co., Ltd., regards public responsibility as a fundamental corporate value, an integral component of everything they do — from marketing to philanthropy. They have been pioneers of cause-related marketing around the world, and in Thailand—with their recent "holiday of a life-time" for 1,400 orphans and their participation in this book project — they continue to demonstrate a strong commitment to this corporate philosophy.

ΨCLUB MED. is perhaps the most prominent of French investments in Thailand. Its "brilliant" US$18 million Club Med Phuket resort, a joint-venture of Club Med and Brilliant Thai Partners, opened in December 1985, a glittering addition to the necklace of 110 Club Med Holiday Villages that now encircle the globe.

italthai ITALTHAI GROUP consists of more than 30 companies, including Thailand's largest civil construction company and largest shipbuilder. The group, which was founded in 1955 by Dr. Chaijudh Karnasuta and Mr. Giorgio Berlingieri, has expanded rapidly to become a leader in manufacturing, trading and hotels. Among the group's hotels is The Oriental.

DIETHELM & CO.,LTD. founded as a small trading company on the banks of the Chao Phya in 1906, is today a leader in the marketing and distribution of food products, pharmaceuticals, consumer goods, and technical equipment. Its travel office, Diethelm Travel, is one of Thailand's largest and most experienced.

 is known throughout the world for its steadfast commitment to advanced research and development, product excellence, service quality, reliability and value. In Thailand, AT & T is helping to serve the public and private sectors' demand for advanced telecommunications and computer technology through the introduction of state-of-the-art fiber optics, information networks, integrated circuits and computerised directory services.

 SAHA-UNION CORP., LTD., listed on the securities exchange of Thailand, is the flagship of the Saha-Union Group which comprises over 30 companies with interests ranging from the manufacture of textile products and footwear to stockbrokerage and financial services. The group's export-oriented policy, augmented by several overseas offices, makes its one of the foremost exporters in Thailand today.

PRESKO PUBLIC RELATIONS COMPANY LIMITED, established in 1961, is Thailand's largest commercial public relations consultancy. PRESKO's success in pioneering professional public relations has been attributed to its strategic mix of local and international thinking. With its highly motivated staff of 80, PRESKO is ready to meet Thailand's evergrowing public relations needs.

Ogilvy & Mather *Advertising* has been synonymous with excellence in advertising all over the world. The company's representatives in Thailand are dedicated to creating big ideas that build businesses. Its unique service, called Ogilvy Orchestration, gives Thai clients an integrated variety of communications services including advertising, direct response, public relations and sales promotions.

Bangkok Post, now in its 41st year as Thailand's leading English-language daily, is a vital editorial voice that is highly regarded throughout Asia. Post Publishing Co. Ltd. is a publicly-owned company that employs about 800 people.

Index

Acknowledgements

Asian Institute of Technology
Ballet de Siam Troupe
Border Patrol Police
Bureau of the Royal Household
Chulalongkorn University
The Customs Department, Ministry of Finance
Department of Labor, Ministry of the Interior
The National Identity Board
The Office of His Majesty's Principle Private Secretary
Royal Thai Army
The Supreme Command Headquarters

Adisorn Charanachitta
Al Eberhardt
Alison Jonas
Alois Fassbind
Amnart Sukteeka
Amporn Samosorn
Angkana Tiranaprakit
Barry Owen
Captain Boonchu Kerdchoke
Captain Phorphol Maneerintr
Captain Thirawat Prapaprasert
Carol Phatoomros
Chalie Amatyakul
Chana Kraprayul
Charnchai Phiromsawat
Chertchai Methanayanonda
Chitdee Rangavara
Chokchai Bulakul
Col. Boonsang Niempradit
Col. Faengphat Boonleing
Col. Somchet Pisitsoontorn
Col. Sornchai Montivat
Col. Surapol Krasaechat
Col. Vacharacharn Phokaew
Col. Visanu Kongsiri

Jacques Bes
James Corcoran
Jay Smith
Jeff Tan
John Seifert
John Ellis
John Owens
Joseph Hart
Julian Spindler

Karnchanee Komkris
Keiko Hiranprueck
Kriengsak Tantiphipop
Kumaree Chinawat
Lalita Na Ranong
Leelanuch Angkavisitphan
Linda Lisahapanya
Louie Morales
Luc Distelmans
M.L. Tuang Snidvongs
M.R. Chirisuda Vuthigrai
Major Monthon Bamrungpruk
Major Pornchai Duangnate
Malcolm Mckenzie-Vass
Mark Graham
Merry Bateman
Narudee Kiengsiri
Nong-Yao Vangcharoen
Noreerat Nopparatnaraporn
Norman Pajasalmi
Norman Brottroff
Phaitoon Khemkhang
Piyatep Canungmai
Ploenpit Han
Pornpan Veravatanadej
Prakit Chinamourphong
Prapaisri Devahastin
Pratin Buranabunpot
Preecha Khunhong
Preecha Sowanna
Presha Ruksakiati
Priyachart Dhevapalin
Puangsri Prachuabdee
Punlert Baiyoke

Ratanavudh Vajarodaya
Renato Petruzzi
Richard Segalowitch
Ron Spaulding
Roonrit K. Dilokrat
Ruenrat Hansakul
Sinn Phonghanyudh
Sirikan Kahattha
Siriwan Hemacha
Somkit Tantadvanichkul
Sompan Charumilinda
Sompong Patpui
Steve Van Beek
Sucharit Bulakul
Sunathee Isvarphornchai
Supak Aksaranukroh
Suphadej Poonpipat
Suriyapa Bunnag
Suvannee Sriduluang
Thavee Chowrungrattanasiri
Tipavarn Thephasdin

Vanee Akasarirk
Varavuth Tulyayon
Vibul Boonbandit
Vinai Suttharoj
Virakiart Angkatavanich
Virat Jirachatrangkura
Virongrong Chanvinij
Wichai Rungjira-Urai
William D. Black
William Booth

Danielle Iwaszkiewicz
David Pratt
Dhanit Siridhara
Dr. & Mrs. Roger Hawkey
Dr. John Yang
Dr. Kalaya Issarasena
Esko Pajasalmi
Flying Off. Boonlert Thavatchai
Geoff Thompson
Gerald Pierce
Gregoire Salamin
H.P. Tuggener
Heinz Braendli
Henry Widler
Ian Fawcett

Pictures on this page by
Bancha Cheunprapanusorn